Table of Cont

Dedication	**Pg 1**
Preface	**Pg 2**
Introduction	**Pg 3**

◆◆◆

Chapters

Perception is not everything... All my Relations... A little help goes a long way...

Speaking of change... Expectations... Nature of the Beast....

Community is Home... The answers will come... A way of record keeping...

Going with the flow. Sometimes quickly, sometimes slowly...

Teachings from Uncle ... If the teaching fits... Working through the fear

Full circle... Voices from beyond... Making the most of it... Spontaneous healing...

Back to the beginning...Getting myself out of the way... Being in the state of...

Kindness really is everything... Fear being the opposite of faith...

Gift from a Hummingbird Relative... That's good stuff...

Gratitude is in the action... Becoming willing... Well, that's just perfect...

I hear you calling... Hope growing from compassion...

Love my Relatives... Figuring it out... Stories shared...Sharing is caring...

◆◆◆

Dedication

To my sons Shawne, Kennith, and Andrew.

Without you, I would not have discovered life.

With love and gratitude All-Ways

◆◆◆

Preface

Once upon a time...we lived in a moment that allowed us to be ever present in the looking after of our good hearts, our good minds, our good bodies, and our good Spirits, we greeted the sun with our wordless prayers of gratitude and willingness to live in the harmony of the day. We then would go about looking after our families, our communities, our selves with food, water, love and a knowing that we were intimately involved in the Ceremony that is life.....we understood our place in the Medicine Wheel and lived accordingly without the pain and suffering that can and has crippled us today.

Take the time during your greeting the sun to see where you are in the circle of balance in your moment...acknowledge what is working for you, what is no longer yours to carry, what does not serve your purpose anymore, thank it all and then let it go, feel the freedom from re-claiming the balance. "Human Beings are comfort junkies. we will do whatever it takes to be comfortable unless the doing of it is uncomfortable." It seems to be the simplest explanation for why I see people including myself not doing whatever it takes at any given time to achieve and stay in the proverbial place of joy, contentment and dare I say enlightenment.

   I find it compelling that although this appears to apply to the mental. Emotional and spiritual aspects of our being, when it comes to the physical however, we have been known to accomplish some pretty awe-mazing feats of endurance, strength, and tenacity. I feel like we are the only Species that has what feels like this self-absorbed inherent characteristic that explains while dictating our way of how we navigate the onslaught of experiences which we step into. All other Beings that roam, fly, slither, and swim have their own set of instinctual behaviors.

Introduction

Traditionally teachings and information sharing were generally handed down through oral means. This was done via story telling. Which was then left up to the listener to take responsibility for how they were going to extract what was wanting to be conveyed.

So, one had to be at the ready for any opportunity. It was never as simple as the gathering of individuals around the knee of the teller in anticipation of being regaled with images of the past conjured up through floral words.

The moment could come in the most unexpected way. like when Grandma while she was canning salmon, would start going down memory lane to the time when she was picking berries across the way.

Within this story there would be reference to the medicines around her, who she was with, what so and so said or did and how the wind or sky had a distinct quality that day creating natures own natural therapeutic opportunity for an aromatherapy session.

It was up to the listener to weave through the many layers and bringing light to the teachings that Grandma was wanting to pass on for the survival of culture, their way of life. Some of the most profound teachings I have been blessed with have come from this way of sharing.

I can still today be in the middle of an experience and suddenly I have what I call a light bulb moment where I am instantly thrown back to when something was shared a few months or even years ago and my brain goes" ah this is what they meant.

Perception is not everything…

Websters, or Mister Googles I have come to call it as of lates definition of an Outlier is such. "a person or thing situated away or detached from the main body or system. A person or thing differing from all other members of a particular group or set." I immediately looked up the word because I loved the way it rolled around in my mouth landing in my throat before making its way through my blood stream to be absorbed by the cells that decided long ago who I was. This moment of clarity hit my mind like a beam of light emanating out from a central, warm comforting space not unfamiliar to my core Being.

I had very recently heard this word for the first time recently and although friends have stated they saw me as grounded and connected, I have always felt apart from…. All my life, starting from the time I muscled up the courage to leave the one physical space I had known to come into this time, I have felt different. Not like those around me.

Not in the way in which society has inadvertently proclaimed the how and the ways in which the method of connection was deemed valid. Felt as if my coming from another planet was the only reasoning as to why these feelings of separateness have been so strong within me at times.

That when I speak out loud to whomever is listening to me through the hidden veil which separates us, me from the full connection experience of the limitlessness consciousness.

The style of language I use in any given scenario has its effect on my essence whether I am fully aware of it or not. Given enough time it will show itself in the reflection of how I think, the environment around me in which I choose to call home, job, friendships, and community. I am learning to "check" myself. Asking myself if is this true. I was going to say "spent most of my better days" but I now feel like I have so many more of those yet those to come so I continue with this.

I have spent most of my days between questioning what was wrong with me and thus attempting to change to fit the exterior mold and telling myself I am me just the way I am, and it feels right. As a result, the path of experiences has lain itself out as such that you will read in the following reminiscing's.

All my Relations...

Back in the late 90s after a brief stint in the recycling department of what used to be Laidlaw Waste management before Canadian Waste bought them out outside Kelowna, I found myself working at the whistler landfill with my most beloved friend, companion, and when I say companion truly that's what he was as he was never far from my side at any given moment for the first 7 years of his life. My four-legged buddy Sarge. The employment opportunity for the both of us presented itself out of sheer luck, or cosmic divinity.

I was chatting it up with the guy that was flushing out the sewage system in our yard. We lived in an old wooden style A frame that looked somewhat like those ski in-ski out cabins one would see in an old James Bond film taking place in some European back country scenario. Yet it was just on the forested edge of Whistler. I had moved here to re-unite with my second husband. Trying one more time to make it work, the last desperate attempt to prove to myself that I was indeed worthy of that forever relationship phase.

To fulfill the reasoning my heart shared in which I so desperately didn't want to be alone, that everything was shiny and new like a newly minted coin, and it would forever stay that way. While still together during one of the previous short-lived attempts in Vernon, my husband and I had retrieved this incredible, most amazing canine from outside the town of Cherryville BC. It was a toss up between him and his sister in the back of an old chevy pick-up truck out on the side of dirt road.

They were both so adorable 8-week-old pups but what attracted me to Sarge was his eyes. Those deep brown eyes followed me everywhere with an awareness that showed much intelligence. I was right. On the way back to Vernon we had to stop to let him do his thing and give him a reprieve from the ride. I'm sure he was a little motion sickness.

We pulled off to the side in the snow by an open half moon treed area. I got out first while my husband kept him in the van. I also wanted to see if he was a tracker. The owner had said his breed was Coyote Collie and Shepard. I made my tracks in a single line around the edge of the woods then veered into them with an eye on the vehicle. Sarge was released. What was evident right away was his keen sense of smell.

He immediately dipped his nose into my first foot track and proceeded to follow my path. Stepping only in my tracks after confirming with scent I had indeed made it. He found me in the trees. So cool!!

After he did his business, it was, he who led us out. Right back the way we came and straight to the van. From that point on I knew he was the one meant for me. Even though both my husband and I chose Sarge together, there was this unspoken acknowledgement between this amazing 4 legged relative and I that we were fulfilling the commitment we made long before we ever set eyes on each other. We spent the first four months together bonding.

I was with him 24/7, no one else fed him, no one outside the family touched him. Eventually he was ready. He worked so hard and was always on alert as to how he could take a cue from me to do whatever I asked. I was quite active in hiking, Wild crafting medicines from Mother Nature the way I was taught and there were many encounters with bears. My goal was to train him as a bear dog. Working at the landfill was the perfect place to start. By the time Sarge was fully ready to work on his own, he had already established a 10-hand signal and 30-word vocabulary. Oh, the stories I could tell of his days there.

Days with what was to be his best bear friend. I called this guy Brute. He was a big ole 15-year-old fella that at any time would be seen running from 16 lb Sarge into the treeline where Sarge would herd him into before pulling back. They of course would also be spotted on more then one occasion grazing amongst the garbage goodies side by each.

At one time Sarge was doing his "duty" and herding Brute out the open gate of the landfills first phase garbage drop off area, across the road and up into the treeline. Keep in mind the size difference between these two and that at any time Brute could have stopped short, turned-on Sarge and with one clean swipe of his powerful paw, take Sarge out.

He didn't however, he had decided to play the "who's the dominant one today game" and continued to do his part. I had needed to stop one of the gravel trucks from the pit down the road so Sarge could do this. So here is this driver watching the whole process shaking his head. He told me later if he hadn't seen it with his own 2 eyes, he would never have believed it!

This most unusual relationship still conjures up memories of a particular Saturday morning bugs bunny cartoon where the sheep dog Ralph and the wolf Sam had this similar working relationship. "Morning Ralph", "Morning Sam "would be the exchange as they punched their timecards clocking in and out.

These two were so close that when Brute was tragically hit by one of the Trucks outside the attendant building one day on our day off, as we came into work the next shift, Sarge knew something was up. His usual opening role after I would tell him "On duty" was to circle the buildings, the trucks, barking to let all creatures great and small know he was there and on watch. But on this day as he was making his way down the road to go behind the first building, he abruptly stopped.

In the middle of the road, he started sniffing intensely. Turns out this was the spot where Brute just 3 days earlier had been hit. Instead of finishing his rounds he came to the door of the attendant station his tone of whine had a soulful cry to it. He then curled himself up on the couch, his head cradled in his outstretched front paws.

The look on his face was so sad. He stayed there grieving for the rest of the day. My heart hurt for him. He knew his buddy was gone.... This would not be the first time I would witness the distinct connection between two different species of our nonhuman relatives in my life. It was a very clear teaching on the concept of what the Lakota term ' Mitakuye Oyasin' " which in general translation means All My Relations.

Going forward with this understanding has really lifted so many perceived ideas for me that have been perpetuated by those who are of the mindset that as human Beings we are superior, the only ones that know all the required information to function in this reality and therefore need to be acknowledged or dare I even say worshipped.

A little help goes a long way....

Recycling has felt like it's always been a daily part of my life even long before it was the cool thing to do. So much so that while I was working at the landfill, on one of my days off I volunteered at what was called Base two. It was midway up Blackcomb Mountain. It was here that all the supposed recycling bags that were gathered daily off both Blackcomb and whistler Mountain was dropped to be dealt with.

While trying to stay warm dancing around from one foot to the other wiggling the toes regularly inside 2 layers of socks stuffed into thin rubber boots in one of those overcrammed shipping containers as my workspace, I would be ripping open, sorting, bagging and categorizing their refundable containers in exchange for a free seasons pass for both Whistler and Blackcomb mountain ski hills.

Through all the "eww" so gross, stinky moments the idea never occurred to me that it just wasn't worth all this. In fact, it was the opposite. I felt like I was in some small way contributing to what was still the new catch phrase of "reducing the carbon footprint."

I still occasionally dream I'm back there when it was a simpler time. My job at the landfill consisted of mostly going through people's "stuff". looking over what they wanted to purge whether from renos, or the what the heck am I still hanging onto this for episodes. Then figure out the fee for doing so and tell them where to dump it.

Now the former part of that statement was where the thirty seconds of politeness was all they could muster was over once they realized that, yes, they did have to pay that extra 10 dollars for the broken bits of drywall they tried to hide in a black plastic garbage bag pretending it was old clothes.

Cheap buggers! Then there were the ones that had more money than common sense. I could not believe the stuff they would get rid of. Like almost brand-new beds, appliances, other furniture.

Fortunately, I've always been a sort of a scavenger at heart, so it only made sense to me to rescue what I could to find better long-term homes for those that not only would appreciate but also for those that needed these items. This organically evolved into the start of the towns first and only small free store for those that welcomed the opportunity to extend the life of still usable goods.

I laugh to this day when I think about that time because during this time myself and a friend of mine who also worked there part time were in the habit of claiming all sorts of items that were in such great condition that we decided to have a garage sale at my place and wouldn't you know it we both made over 200.00 selling the towns inhabitants stuff back to them that they had at some point rid themselves of. We even overheard a couple individuals' comment "Hey, I used to have one just like this!" Bahahaha!

The free store was later shut down once I was no longer there but because of it existence even for a short while, the Pique newspaper did a 2-page feature on how it came about, the purpose it served and the people it helped. Whistler could no longer pretend that it did not have people in need. It was finally time for them to admit there was another side to this Disneyland that operated by its own book of rules. As a result of the attention, they begrudgingly started a Re-use it Store. The first Rebuild it store came later.

So popular was this Thrifters dream place that in a very short period was financially contributing to 27 community services along the Sea to Sky corridor. YAY!! Some of the most common questions I still get asked when I talk about my time of employment there is "how could you stand the smell" and "didn't it ever get boring?" I had quickly become" nose blind" long before the term was a common commercial phrase. As for boring or lonely, that was never an issue at the landfill. Alongside me were some of the local 4 footed furry residents.

There was a constant circle of coyotes that would regularly send out their best female howling out pretending to be injured to try and lure Sarge their way. He was too smart for that trick though. After Brute had crossed over, his preens was replaced by a big ole black bear that had to have been 300 to 400 lbs at the least. Part of his routine was to frequent our glass recycling section out the back behind the shop where all the drivers had their trucks and their own office.

We had a large concrete slab surrounded on 3 sides with interlocking cement blocks where they dumped all the glass recycling that was picked up from around the village.

Part of my job as the landfill attendant was to go through the glass before it would be transferred by front end loader to a huge bin to be trucked further back behind the landfill to the local gravel pit. Which meant picking out the contaminants and non glass items people would throw into the bins. Directly out the door the first thing I saw was a concrete block wall that separated my view from anything happening on that slab until I came around the one side of it. So, I usually heard him before I saw him. I always tried not to startle him because A; I didn't want him to lunge at me and B most importantly scare him, causing him to break out into a run across the broken glass adding further harm to this black beauty of nature.

It was not unusual to see spots of blood that came from the inevitable gashes from this hazardous food gathering technique. He was not just what people would label a garbage bear as my work was not his only source of food.

This was just a pitstop for him before he would wash down his meal with a few branches of the Mountain Ash berries from the small trees lining the forested area surrounding the work site. When I saw how he would crawl all over through the broken glass, it would bring up so much of my own stuff about wanting to rescue him, take over the reigns of natures own plan, to feed him. But common sense would inevitably prevail.

I would sometimes for a moment before tossing something his way or shouting to startle him off, stand at a safe distance watching him push his snout in and about. Digging out week old unwashed jars coated with moldy spaghetti sauce attached to the shards. This behavior seemed not unlike the tactic used for hunting up grubs hidden under a rock at the base of a rotting tree stump.

What was even more astonishing was that this bear appeared to have either a broken or maybe deformed front right leg. It would teeter, trying to balance the large frame while dragging the unusable attachment along with him as it was trying to add every ounce of weight to its frame. At the time I felt for it because in my judgy mind it was suffering while making do with what was handed to him without self-pity, complaint, or surrender. Just in a matter of fact doing what needed to be done kind of way while making it through as the circumstances dictated.

25 years later it has occurred to me that time and time again as I have had to move on with my own business of surviving, getting on with it whatever "IT" was I have unwittingly taken a page from this brave, charismatic forest dwellers book. More times in my life then I card to remember I had lived hand to mouth, paycheck to paycheck as a single mom t so when my brain saw an opportunity to earn an extra dollar, I was in there like my brother the bear. There was not only beer and pop cans, but a lot of refundable glass mixed in.

This money glass as I called it was just going with all the other glass to be crushed, so after work I would collect and bag it up to take it to the town Return It Centre to cash in. I then donated the proceeds to my personal earn a living cause. I called it another creative employment opportunity. I figure I added an extra $300-500 a month to my ability to survive another month in a resort town fund. After my time with the landfill was done, I decided that between what I had been able to glean and what was still uncollected in the other commercial garbage deposits that there had to be a better way to intercept it.

So, I started my own recycling business called Heidis Helping Hands in which I took on 27 hotels and restaurants as clients. I would pick up their refundable products, sort them and cash them in to the Return It depot and the local Liquor store. They in turn, depending on how much work I had to do at my end would get a percentage of the money. My minimum fee was 50%.

To put it into perspective how lucrative this new business was, to start all I had was a chevy van to do my pickups and drop offs and within the first 10 months of operation I grossed 67,000! Mind you I started the business in the fall, so it didn't hurt that the busiest time in the resort was just around the corner, coupled with the fact I was not afraid of hard work which during peak times was pretty much 7 days a week until slow down after spring break

Eventually I was able to get the clients to also start recycling some of their nonrefundable containers of tin, glass, and plastic. My business eventually went from not only recycling to support myself and the one son still at home with me but included utilizing my truck for free to re-distribute furniture that the hotels would want gone when they upgraded their rooms but also the daily pick up of day-old goodies from one of the bakeries and giving them away in the community of MT Currie where I lived.

Being able to do this filled my desire to be of purpose, that I was doing something worthwhile and contributing to the community, helping the environment but the work was so physical and methodic that while sorting, organizing etc., it helped me manage what I would later call the OCD side of my personality. I was constantly amazed how not only time would disappear but all the chatter, the craziness in my head would become still once I got into the groove of it all.

If you haven't guessed already there is a definite pattern of stories within a story. For context? Not sure. My dad used to say when I was explaining something to him, he used to say, "I didn't ask for a song and dance." Hahahaha! And its not just me, our whole family does this. An outsider can get easily confused or frustrated when amongst more then 2 of us at the same time. When us sisters get together whether be one on one or as a group, subtexts, meanderings down another topic starts flying, I always thought about inserting a flashcard saying, "topic change!"

◆◆◆

Speaking of change...

Up until now I had often assumed that my whole life's existence was only to be about just getting through one challenging episode after another without any logical reasoning or significance.

It made me ask whoever was listening, the Universe or empty air why was this happening and if this is all there is to my existence what the hell is my purpose here anyways. I was hesitant to put an actual name to the Entity. Didn't want to incur any more wrath if I got it wrong. Because of exposure to various religions, I was convinced there was something, but this "someone" was standing up there with the per functionary clipboard with my name on it and every time I screwed up, He was jotting it down for the record mumbling to himself that I was in for it when I got there.

Every now and again though, possibly for the sake of a breather? life sprinkled brief moments of time that carried with it so much calm, like a feeling of phew I got through that one in my chest, that I would float around almost in a manic state with the confidence of the most assured.

The confidence that I was living, breathing, finally succeeding in the manner with which the Universe intended. This presented itself in the way of so many kinds of jobs that would propel me forward to either a new home, town, province, or relationship. The ole geographical cure. Albeit temporary as hand in hand I was being accompanied by what I thought for many years was my friend, the Drink.

When I was around 11, I had my first taste of what I had come to learn was but a symptom of a mental, emotional, and spiritual dis-ease. That was the introduction of alcohol and its natural warming that flowed through my young body. This body glow instantaneously sent a message to my brain that I had finally found even in my short life exactly what I thought was missing. I would later in recovery learn the inner longing came from the place that was my essence, my heart.

However, until such time of clarity and understanding came about in sobriety, all I knew for sure was that that first sip propelled me into an almost 20-year active addiction that required me to chase and try to replay that feeling of warmth that spread throughout me as the sweet sickly taste of Green Crème de Mint slid down my throat.

In the beginning of my sobriety while my sponsor and I were going through the steps, talking about this whole Higher power God idea, I shared the deep fears surrounding that which I had carried around. She said," If you were going to put an ad in the paper for a Higher Power, what would they need to have on their resume to qualify in the application process? I want you to create an ad like this and put it somewhere in your home where you will see it daily." She was always giving me "homework" when we would meet. when she gave me my latest task my mind was open enough that I connected with that idea immediately and drafted up a want ad posting it on my fridge.

Every time I looked at it helped me to find a way to replace the old idea of a punishing Being. Over time it worked and today I genuinely feel I have this relationship with a most kind, compassionate, nonjudgemental Creator that only wants the best for me, my family, for all of us that take a breath.

The first time however when we met to get a sense of who we each were and whether we would be a good fit, she told me "Part of my job as your sponsor will be giving you homework. This will be done on time with no excuses short of you being in the hospital or broken wrists and can't write.

If its not done, you will be fired." I was like in my mind "do you know who you're talking to? I don't need this. "Of course, the ego.

This other Self was a fighter. It knew that any time there was change and personal growth coming that would healing my Spirit. It meant there would be less and less opportunity for its survival. It lived in fear of that. Of losing its say, its control. After I calmed down, I agreed. I mean in my drinking days to survive I manipulated, conned, and tried to control every situation I found myself in. I needed someone to call me on my stuff. The ole "there now dear, everything will be alright" accompanied with a pat on the back wasn't going to keep me sober.

Slowly but surely, I learned to do the things that were suggested and the life I knew outside of my head started to change. My world before 30 was so unapologetically insane that as I look back now and try to piece the sequencing and rationale of it all I just shake my head in disbelief that it all crammed itself into a very short period.

Was it remotely possible that I made some of this up or dreamt it? It felt like I was at times reading someone else's story. Confirmation of it all would be presented itself to me through the evidence of destruction and mayhem that lay strewn in my path. When I was clear about it, I had convinced myself that I must have inherited from some relative in the asylum in Alberta the same genetic defect that would end me up in a similar scenario. I mean really who exists like that and isn't touched in the head?? I hadn't yet understood that definition of insanity that you are familiar with that says " doing the same thing over and over again yet expecting different results is insanity"

Cleaning up my act not only enabled me in the beginning to go back to school to get my GED. But opened the door for me to experience being a carpet installers helper, working with concrete doing foundations. Field hand on an organic farm. Stocked shelves in a grocery store. Stacked them high in produce section.

Did landscape construction for someone else before venturing out on my own and was able to obtain official education as a Certified Natural Health Practitioner which not only enabled me to work in health food stores at various levels but to develop my own client list.

As a matter of fact, when I moved to the community of Mt Currie (more on that transition later) It was the perfect place to do trades. I worked with community members to support their individual issues and in exchange they provided me with sockeye salmon for my smoker, deer meat and moose hides for the drum making workshops I would run.

Part of this new to me way of living also created its own times of self-induced chaos until many years later it and when I say it, I really mean me, I leveled out. Sobering up did not come with ready-made ingrained skills, however. I had to learn how to be a healthy sister, daughter, employee, friend, and a mother.

This of course did not happen overnight and honestly; I am still evolving as some of them to this day. As a result, there are most definitely various decisions, choices that I I made which have had long lasting irreparable repercussions not only for me but for my sons. Some of these most painful have taken a couple of decades to forgive myself for.

 Even then pending on the day whether I am in balance in my wellness wheel pretty much dictates said level or degree if you will of self forgiveness. I feel like it seems so much easier to forgive others. Maybe because there has been closure of sorts with them.

Expectations....

 I married and unmarried for a second time in sobriety. Two complete opposite wedding styles with two entirely different kinds of men but both ending in the same way. Divorce. Now that either says something about my choice in men or as I would hope to see it, that I was growing and evolving.

The first was pre-sober days to my youngest boy's father. I allowed him to pick me up one night during one of my shifts at a bar I was working in. He fit the requirements.

 Drank like I did, could play a mean John Fogerty/ CCR on the lead guitar, was handsome. Didn't object to me already being a single parent and he had a job. Back then there was no Tinder or any other online options for possible mates. Except maybe E-Harmony was around. This union would be playing a major part in the final downward spiral into the depths smacking face first into what was known as the bottom of my alcoholism/ drug addiction phase.

When they say like attracts like, with him it was not only what we presented to each other, but I think our inner scars that we both consciously and unconsciously worked hard at pretending didn't exist were also major factors in our union. It also was a huge contribution as to our lasting together if we did despite our blatant habit of blaming each other whenever the natural and logical consequences of out individual and collective actions rained down on us. It was almost as if every time our life was running on an even keel one of us would shift in some way that sabotaged the very joy and fulfillment, we both so desperately wanted.

It didn't help that a lot of these moments were spurred on and supported by the distorted thinking brought on by the heavy participation of our addictions.

Those times where our sincere deep love for each other did shine through though often enough which led me to believe the voice inside my head whispering "this time things will be different." One of these times was when we finally decided to get married. Getting caught up in the hoopla of planning and such. Solidifying a father figure for my two older boys.

The youngest hadn't made the decision to join us in this realm yet. I remember picking out my wedding dress from the second-hand store. It was this elegant pearl coloured oriental style mid calf length dress with short sleeves. by this stage in my life, I had acquired my first 2 forearm tattoos and I wanted to cover them.

So, my friend and neighbour down the hall of our apartment building offered to take some of the material off the bottom and make fingerless gloves that ran up to the inside of the elbows. I felt like a queen dressed that day.

The wedding ceremony was a civil one conducted by a Justice of the Peace in his home with my dad giving me away and my boys alongside the JPs wife as witnesses. I look back on one picture of the four of us and one son was obviously not a happy camper with the events of the day. When I finally made the decision to leave him, I was 3 months sober.

It wasn't because I didn't love him anymore but because we were going in different directions, and it seemed the whole time I was with him I put him above my children in many ways and the consequences of that finally shook me out of the last bit of fog called denial as to my addictions.

With him still drinking and using and me newly on this clean and sober path, I felt so very deep in my heart that if we stayed together, I would relapse and the excruciating soul pain I experienced that caused me to get it together in the first place, well, I could not, I would not ever risk be going through that ever again. Sadly, he was never able to find the path of a better life and after a long battle with serious health repercussions because of continuing to use, he crossed over.

He has however shown up on occasion taking care of me and his son. I have felt his comforting arms holding me in the night. Have felt him in the home watching over his son. Quite different the second marriage. This one in Sobriety was the full-on church wedding, limousine, honeymoon with all the extras adding to the memories of such a treasured time. There I was what felt like floating down the isle in a custom-made lace trimmed white mermaid style dress.

Despite the air of excitement and anticipation amongst the guests, I knew before I even got halfway up that isle that I was making a mistake. I did not have however the courage to walk away.

My mind kept telling me how much I would let everyone down who came. And of course, what I think was the most delusional thought originating from watching too many romance movies, I would learn to love him in the way marriage was meant to be about. It would be a huge waste of all money I had spent. I willingly did so but really shouldn't have. Not long before our decision to make our union as legal as it could get, I had received a settlement of sorts which I guess thinking about it now the main reason I released it so freely was because the monetary retribution I received felt like blood money, and I couldn't get rid of it fast enough.

After buying some long wanted items for myself and the boys, impulse buys, gave away various amounts to some family members, of course spent a pile on the wedding. Our bridal registry was at Valhalla sports equipment because in this chapter of my journey I was paired with a man whose whole life revolved around adventure sports and I unconsciously started to mold my interests, hobbies to fit his. Ignoring once again the opportunities to explore who I was.

Don't get me wrong though I am extremely grateful for him as I learned how to ski, mountain terrain hiking, bivouacking under the stars on a glacier snow packed ridge, as well as rock climbing.

When we were first dating, or should I say living together because the good little co-dependent in me rescued and moved him into the boys and my space within weeks of our first date. He had developed a severe respiratory infection and was at the time living in a cabin on the lake middle of winter with no electricity and only wood stove for heat. So, I convinced him my abode would be a better recovery spot.

And of course, one thing led to another…Anyways one day he took me out to one of his favorite and popular climbing spots that overlooked Kalamalka lake, just outside of Vernon, for my first lesson. It was a simple top rope with a rating of 6.7 which is what the experts would call easy.

After getting all the gear set up and the rope hung, he positioned himself at one end of the rope on Belay, with me harnessed into the other end with the middle fed through a couple of carabiners attached to anchors at the top. I was excited!! Off I go.

lifting myself off the ground by handholds made from cracks and weirdly shaped rock jutting along the route until I was about a quarter of the way up. He was sitting on the ground leaning back keeping the tension on the rope, so I didn't swing about like a spider losing its place on its line. Like I said I'm a quarter way up when I take a moment to finally breath and look around at the view. First mistake. The first mistake was moving too quickly without a break.

The second was looking away from the rock and suddenly realizing how high up off the ground I was. I knew I had issues with heights, but this view had paralyzed me. My arms and legs instantly developed the inability to move while simultaneously my insides started shaking with sweat pouring off my brow into my eyes and soaking my hands so badly, I thought I was going to lose my grip on the rock wall which in my imagination would cause my body to plummet rapidly to the ground. I cried to hubby "I'm sorry! I can't do this!!"

His response as he laughed was "What are you sorry to me for, you're the one stuck up on the rock!" If I was scared before, now I'm most definitely upset. Within minutes my limbs thawed, and I literally raced to the top, pulled myself over the edge of the face and collapsed onto the ground. I had tears running down my face and snot dripping out of my nose. I wasn't even aware I was crying.

After rolling onto my back to catch my breath, I was like Holy crap! I did it!! Expectations are pre-meditated resentments. Let me say that again.... Expectations are pre-meditated resentments. I had learned to change my expectations. Of self and of others. Cause in any experience I'm the one that can be "stuck on the rock". Don't be apologetic, just do something. Anything to get moving. Forwards backwards it doesn't matter. Please just don't stand still.

Nature of the Beast....

It was becoming more evident that my doing the same thing repeatedly and expecting different results, that the repetitive behavior trying to implement some of the same survival skills, even not as useful as they once were, were not bringing about the results I wanted. Maybe time to start applying some of the new concepts I've heard from the different people I have had healing conversations with.

Unfortunately, it felt like this understanding would not carry any weight until it traveled from what some would say, a 6-mile path from the head to the heart, it would only remain at the forefront of the mind until another thought came to push it aside eventually. I wasn't used to nor if I'm being honest that practised in creating a peaceful space in my chest for the landing. I can still very easily cling to the familiar. It didn't matter that it was becoming less and less productive to my evolution and growth.

The gift however has to this day been that these episodes of the old ways happen less frequently and don't have as long a stay as they used to.

Still though, once again, I decided to relocate. Yes, I am aware that this too was an old tool. Starting fresh though always seemed to take the edge off a bit and give the illusion that I was doing great.

Community is Home….

I ended up in a first nations community called Mt Currie that sits in the unceded territory of the Lil'wat peoples. They, being some of the different community members, after watching me from afar, eventually opened their homes, culture, and families.

They allowed me to refer to their ways of addressing them as Sister, Brother Auntie and Uncle. This most honest, authentic, and raw place of existence that was mostly tucked in behind the cluttered yards that surrounded homes in dire need of some physical refurbishing is where I finally called home. I claimed it as such not just by the moving in of furniture into a Pana boat cabin on main street but also with my heart. To this day when I talk of home the connection, I have been granted, to this land is where I mean.

Back in the early days, a logging company brought in the made to look like a log cabin I lived in and a few others like it to Mt Currie by way of floating them down the Lillooet River, then barging them in over the Lillooet Lake before setting in place on the main road.

And with that came the first road carved out which created a thoroughfare that eventually made its way from over the Mountain known as the Duffy Lake Road to whistler and further. This would eventually become part of the Sea to Sky highway.

I spent six years in this space, Finding my way around the territory. Learning firsthand not only about their culture, but also the gift of seeing up close how this strong resilient community was not only surviving the daily generational pain and suffering some were experiencing, but that these authentic, kind, welcoming, genuine peoples were thriving.

Despite the horrendous footprints left behind in the hearts and minds in many community members by Residential School trauma, this was/is a resilient lineage of peoples.

Out of respect for the People, I choose not to elaborate on this part of their journey as it is not my story to tell.

Since the only source of heat, me and the youngest son relied upon was a big old wood stove in the corner of the living room, with my trusty 357 Husqvarna chainsaw with an 18" bar in the back of my compact chevy pick-up truck, I spent many hours most days off from spring to fall gathering the next winters firewood. Scoping out the old logging roads up the mountains for the burn piles that were left behind from the commercial loggers. The wood was not valuable enough for market, but it worked simply fine for our little abode.

So, after using my little whisk hand broom to clean off the section where I would make the cut, a trick one of my friends that worked at the pole yard in Mt Currie building log homes taught me in his tutorial of chainsaw maintenance, I'd buck it up then bring it home. Me or my son would toss it off the back of the truck where he would then split and stack it. Usually after school.

When needed he would make kindling and bring that with an armful of the split into the house. Even though the whole searching, gathering and the bringing home of the firewood was very physically demanding at times, I really enjoyed it. It felt like I was being productive in looking after my son, myself, and our home. And as we all know the bonus of listening to that crackle of the flames even when cannot see them is so soothing to the spirit. I eventually started to also "make wood," the expression of getting firewood used by the local members of the community, for some of them as well. There were so many that also relied on wood for their source of heat but did not have the means to get it. For those that relied on others to get their wood, the band office would give them a firewood slip.

This slip would be filled out by both the receiver and the person who brought the wood load and handed into the band office. Once a month all slips under the person or company who delivered the wood, would get paid. The ones that had this job were also members of the Mt Currie band but because I had been living in the community for a couple years now and was becoming known to them, the Band office decided one year to include me as a payable source. I was doing it for free in the beginning anyways because it was important to me to look after the Elders when and how I could.

They truly felt like my Grandmas, Grandpas, and Aunties. The plus side of having the time and energy to be selective where I got the wood at various times was, I was able to have access to most wood others left behind because the size was too small for them. For me though the sizes were just perfect for the stoves of the ones I gathered for. No splitting was needed. This was good.

I wanted to make sure those I gathered for did not need to rely on waiting for someone to take care of that for them. Which realistically could be days or weeks. One day I was up a cut block by myself as usual cutting rounds and throwing them in the back when this truck came into sight from above.

I looked to see who was driving because there was always a chance someone you knew was doing the very same thing. I did not recognize the driver, but he was also having a good look at and around me. He slowly came to a stop and leaned out his window." You out here by yourself?' he asked as if he expected at any moment a man to appear out from behind a tree after relieving himself. "Yep" I replied. He then proceeded to give me all sorts of what he felt were helpful tips on using the saw and such. I did not bother to let him know I had already been schooled a couple of years before by a good friend who worked at a pole yard building log cabin.

He then mentioned that if I wanted a real viable choice of wood, that I should head up where he had come from as they were Heli logging there. As our conversation was wrapping up another vehicle made its way down to where we were and as if on cue the driver asked" are you out here by yourself?" I laughed as the first guy said" I just asked her that." Nice of them to be concerned though.

The answers will come....

Just before I moved "home" in 2000, I was attending what had become my regular Sunday cleansing sweat lodge Ceremony in Mt Currie, a Reserve 38km drive from Whistler. While we were sitting outside the lodge waiting for the Grandfathers in the fire to be ready, I was asked how life was going. I immediately launched into a ramble of situations that was not as I thought they should be. "Whistler is such a party town; "I don't feel like I belong there. The activities I enjoy are more centered outside of it.

The practise of Ceremony and the people I connect with are all out this way. "On and on I went. Note to Self: when in Ceremony whether in the Lodge itself or outside of it, the Fire, the Spirits hear you. Be careful of your thought's words and actions. It was shared with me that the minute you make the conscious decision to go to ceremony, in their realm, the ceremony has already begun, and they start to prepare.

Within 3 weeks of that sweat, I ended up with a 3-month eviction notice. Despite every effort made to stay where my work was would you believe the only place I could find was on the Main drag of Mt Currie! The very place I traveled regularly to soothe my Spirit. wander the forested areas in and around gathering medicines the way I was taught and participate in community events.

The place where I would connect in the most profound way with its community members who Creator saw fit to bring me onto the path of the Sundance. I was now developing a faith in the good Creator, the Universe as it were that enabled me to see and trust what the next step was as it made itself clear. By this time in my life too many things were happening in such a way that could not be explained away as a coincidence. It was shared with me once that when the Creator is directing us a certain way, the messages will come in groups of 4.

Take ending up at the Sundance sweat lodge (which was different the medicine lodge I had been frequenting). This lodge I was told was on what was referred to as "across the way" by the community. Also known as the old reserve tucked away on some land by the river. So off I went to try and find it. The goal at the time was just to support the other Sun dancers in the community. I wandered, I kid you not up and down that rivers shore looking into the trees and fields 6 or 7 times over a few months, and do you think I could find it? Not a chance.

Then one day there I was, sitting with them waiting for the grandfathers in the fire to tell us when it was time to go in. Don't ask me how I got there nor who took me there. To this day when I think of it, it's like I was just there. I have no memory of who took me there, anything about the lead up to it. Not long after this time that I went from being a supporter to pledging to dance for 4 years myself. How did I know this was meant for me? I received a couple different messages from Source. The first one was a dream, the second was an experience at the fire.

We were in between rounds at the sweat and a couple of the guys were teasing another non-indigenous man that had already danced his first year with them. They were joking and laughing about how when it came time for him to break off his ropes off the Tree he just kept bouncing when he tried to pull back. It was like he had chicken skin. As they told it two male leaders had to take him on each side and pull his body back with enough force to finally allow the cherry sticks attached to the ropes on his chest to tear the skin and set him free.

As they were describing how he was hanging in the air arms back like outstretched wings by his side I had a flash! I suddenly had a flashback. When I was 9 living with my grandma from my dads side in the big metropolis of Rimbey Alberta. I had had this dream. In this dream/vision I was in what looked like a school portable, but it was very narrow and lined with television screens along the upper part of the walls.

On one of these screens was an image of a man. A white man, bare chested in mid air with his arms spread out like the afore mentioned bird wings and there were two ropes from his chest extending into the air. His head was back, and I could see this long mustache that not only covered his top lip but down the sides to meet his jawline.

This was the man that was sitting in front of me whom the guys were having a go with.!!! The third was just before I made the decision to pledge. I was down at the lodge by myself preparing the area for the dancers cleansing sweat. It was the fourth day after they had broken their fast. Part of the commitment to Sundance was every Thanksgiving and Easter one had to fast for 4 days, no food no water. No brushing of teeth, washing oneself, or other comfort frills. Just go within, take a good honest look at what was no longer necessary to carry and pray about it.

This was done I was told by our Sundance Chief to help us as we entered the arbor, be in a heart space of celebration, not suffering. Over the years when fasting was brought up some people's response was "what no food or water!!"

I had not been transferred the rights yet to prepare the sacred fire, so my contribution was cleaning out the lodge from last ceremony, cutting kindling and a general clean-up around the site. It was always particularly important to me to do this. It felt like if the area in which our connection with Source was a mess, it was like we had no respect for the process, protocols, or teachings of this way of prayer.

While I was waiting for them to arrive, I was sitting on the east side of the lodge tuning in with Creator, nature and the silence that surrounded me, contemplating whether I should pledge when this huge black bear comes out of the wild rose bushes behind the lodge from the north, stops and looks right at me, continues to the south and before He disappeared into more bushes.

He took one last look at me for a moment as if to say" do you get it yet? "All I could think of was WOW! What a gift. He was so beautiful! His fur was glistening, and he looked so healthy with a glow around him. An Elder from Alberta down south had told me once that sometimes when a spirit comes to us in an animal form, they look like this, larger than the usual, extremely healthy, with an aura of light seemingly around them. The 4th and final message happened that very same day.

I realized I had forgotten my sweat dress and towel, so I headed down to walk the tree-lined dirt road to the highway home. As I was walking, I was reviewing in my mind the bear experience only an hour ago. I sent one more ask to the Creator "are you sure?"

Within seconds I heard what I thought was a rustle and when I turned to look behind me coming up the dirt road just a few feet above me was the hugest owl I had ever seen in my life with a wingspan from tip to tip that had to have been at least 6 feet. As it flew over me it cut the silence with this woosh sound created by its wings moving the air. I turned forward watching it continue, but it just disappeared into nothingness as if it passed through the veil into another realm.

Well, I guess that's it then, I was prepared to commit in the lodge that night. It ended up being canceled, am not sure why but the following Sunday I Pledged.

This pledge led to an active 14-year commitment to not just dance for myself and my family but to be there holding space for the women that were stepping into their own commitments as well on the path.

A way of record keeping….

After coming back from Thailand in 2013 where I took Thai massage training, I embarked on a split career. When it was slow season in Whistler, I lived in my first own home, a 27ft Bonair travel trailer under an open barn on 6acres of land between Pemberton and Mt Currie. Here I had the honor after sitting with Uncles for almost 15 years was given the rights(consent) by them to put up my own sweat lodge.

Where I experienced my most treasured memory of that time was being able to share that most sacred space with one of my nephews. When I wasn't tending to my own garden growing tobacco for ceremony, I was canning on an outdoor fire whatever was in season at the time. I worked in a local health food store in Pemberton. (more about that later).

When the town was crawling with tourists, I would close the trailer and rent a room in whistler from beginning November until end of March. I worked at some of the best as well as a couple of the dodgiest Spas doing massage. Many revelations I will say. Turns out I was not the only one battling with feelings of unworthiness and pain that I focused my energies helping others.

Unfortunately, as it will happen when we don't deal with our own stuff first it doesn't matter how many "others" we help, the unresolved will seep out of our pores manifesting into behaviors that repeatedly caused me to say to myself "how in the hell can they profess to be "healers when they treat each other so badly." The lateral violence, the scheming to manipulate the Spas guest receptionist into taking treatments away from one and other.

However, I had some of the most genuine, kind, authentic famous people as clients that I was able to spend time with. A few that lets just say how they were portrayed in their screen roles was exactly the kind of person the were in real life. I made an incredible amount of money that I didn't have a clue how to budget.

I often feel like there should be a very in-depth course in high school that not only teaches how to do things like get hydro hooked up etc, but also pay the bills while saving for retirement. Now I am aware that the last thing teenagers think about is their own mortality but the whole contributing to the federal retirement programs to be looked after later deal does not have you ending up taken care of financially. When it comes to claiming your federal funds you so diligently albeit required contributed to, its barely enough to pay basic bills and do that other luxury act called eating.

I had spent so many years hand to mouth before this, so mistakes in purchases were made on more than one occasion. However, participating in what I call Ink Therapy was not one of them.

It became a must. Over the years my desire to record meaningful moments on my body through the art of the Tattoo was a most precious way for me to maintain connection. From the first poke of the sewing needle wrapped in thread depicting what this know it all 14-year-old mind of mine thought was the love of my life initials in a heart, to the application of the steady hum of the electric multi needles. Creating a permanent showing of my love for my grandson's names in their Japanese language on my calves was essential. The oldest has an introverted nature and appears to be in a constant state of deep thought carrying an aura about him that equates to that of an old soul. So, I chose to enshrine his Japanese name with a temple and garden.

The younger one however, the exact opposite of his brother. He is fearless it seems, very outspoken and outgoing. The short time I did spend with him when he was little left me with a behavioral reference to a tsunami. His Japanese name translates to Ocean Man, so it is fitting that it is wrapped in the waters white capped waves.

There are also depictions of Cultural images in various anatomical spaces that when asked about I would share my commitment to my belief in their story. When my nephew died by suicide all of us sisters decided to get a tattoo to honor him. For me it was a rose because he used to draw these black and white comics that one might feel a bit gothic but in the corner of one page after he had passed, I noticed this rose with a falling petal for the very first time. I got the rose on my leg.

On my left shoulder blade, I have an indigenous style Sun Tattoo and lower right side of back in the same style a combination that represents the Butterfly, Salmon, and Bear peoples. My first big piece.

In my 4th year of Sundance just after the Tree of life went up in the arbor, some of us were gathered back at our camp doing last minute preparations for sunrise the next day. I was still in my ceremonial dresswear and the moccasins one of my Mt Currie sisters had made for me.

While we were chatting my partner at the time asked once again what the meaning was when a butterfly touched you was. It was shared with me long ago that when a butterfly touches you it is like a kiss from Creator.

I no sooner relayed this when, I kid you not, a butterfly came out of what seemed like nowhere, touched upon the sun beaded on the tops of each of my moccasins before flying into my tent!

 A couple weeks later this blessing was followed up while I was at work mowing lawns in a cul de sac. My tactic was to do a yard on one side then cross the street and do the next yard on the other. As I was approaching the next front yard, mower still on, I noticed on the grass a very still yellow Tigar swallowtail butterfly. I thought it was dead.

I let go of the handle of the mower which automatically turned it off. I reached down slowly with my hand palm up towards this being. It proceeded to crawl onto my hand. I was so awed I held my breath as I stood up. Not wanting to scare it away. My workmate was just up the street, so I decided I wanted to share this beautiful gift with her. As I walked towards her, I brought my butterfly hand towards my chest and without warning it latched itself onto my shirt right at my heart!!! I was astounded. tears of joy welled up in my eyes considering not only because I was still very raw from ceremony but the recent butterfly encounter just a couple weeks previous. I had already decided after Sundance that I wanted to get a tattoo that represented my experience there and this confirmed the notion.

Of course, the person that was to perform this came into my life within weeks. She was an older woman who was doing ink work out of her home having recently finished her training. One of the things that attracted me to the idea of allowing her to do the work was she only used organic ink. Meaning it all was made from bugs and plants. In my first meeting with her I shared the butterfly story so's as to have her understand the depth of this commitment for me. After a few more weeks she had a drawing ready for me to view. I loved it!

The butterfly image had metamorphosized into a combination of itself with the salmon and bear teeth. That year I had attended what was to be the first of 4 year sweat lodge ceremonies to honor the Salmon in hopes to help them strengthen their journey back to the territory. There was also the commitment to not consume any as well.

 The numbers were becoming increasingly low. As for the Bear acknowledgement, I had become acquainted with the teachings of the many ways in what our brother the bear represented. I had also in the last year been given the rights to the bear processing of bear grease out of this creatures' fat for various medicinal and ceremonial purposes.

 I instinctively understood the significance of this trio. It took 3 sessions at 5 hours a piece to complete the work with I will say a regular amount of pain when the needles would vibrate against my spine, rib and shoulder blade but it was worth it. During those times I would lay there focusing on my breath and enter that place of meditation in its purpose.

 By the time I was 58, I had coverage on the back, forearms, and lower legs. Lots of open real estate left though. When the time comes, I will visit once again my favorite artist Dennis in Victoria BC. He has been providing what I like to call Ink Therapy in his dads' shop since he was 17. He not only has helped me create exactly what I was thinking each time. I carry upon my body 7 pieces of his fine work including the cover-ups and touch ups of older poor choices has been amazing!

◆◆◆

Going with the flow….

While working in the high-end Spas, I had inadvertently become of the mindset that there would always be more of the financial wealth shared with me. Regrettably as a result I didn't put anything substantial away for retirement. Only to get me through the next couple of years. Then a succession of physical injuries happened. Followed by COVID.
 In the latter part of 2019 while doing massage in one of the most elite Spas in Victoria BC, I suffered frozen shoulder in my right shoulder.

By the time it had worked its way through, meaning by the time I had adapted my functional activities to the point where I felt I had recovered, it flared up in the left shoulder. Following that after almost two and a half years at my next job, was the back injury at work. Geez, Are you kidding me! Insert emoji of hand slapping forehead while shaking in disbelief

Sometimes quickly, sometimes slowly….

The time of the Pandemic and how this worldwide crisis that although isolated us in so many ways, earned its place of notoriety alongside the "dirty thirties" which ironically bound us together. It felt like a mass participation in a horrible dream where once awakened, the memories of it still so vivid that we can't shake it. Not only are we not shaking it, we have developed a whole way of integrating descriptions while sharing in our conversations by using the phrases "before the pandemic and since .."

 Didn't stop me from moving again though. For some unknown reason I didn't have the awareness or panic that others already were having. As a result of the habit of spontaneously picking up and touching down somewhere else thinking when it happened so smoothly that it was Creators will for me, off again I went. Thinking about that now I realize there was a pattern every two years to different homes, sometimes towns or cities, towns, and of course jobs. The idea of exploring new intimate relationships however was off the table. I never professed to be a fast learner. This moves reasoning was quite legitimate though.

Each time the mom in my heart vibrated so loudly that I needed to come to the mainland from the island on a regular basis to visit my sons. To sedate the yearnings of being able to share my love with them down to a dull roar. It was becoming increasingly challenging for all of us. To be able to co-ordinate work schedules, funds for travel and visit, and being able to find a place to stay while there. The only logical answer was to move back.

From 2019 into the time of the COVID a rapid continuous succession of physical injuries started to happen with me, coincidently alongside these injuries I discovered there was still some well-rooted long-standing ideas in my mind. What was still my core way of coping.

I subconsciously still believed in a few of those old ways. even though I thought I had grown and moved on from, I fell back into them quite readily. Albeit subtly at first. It really didn't occur to me to try anything else.

The only difference that I could see on the surface was that the "old" way of me came out not as often as before and didn't seem to last as long with each episode. Upon reflection on the other side of it, it told me that the foundation I had eagerly built in the first years of sobriety was starting to crumble due to lack of continuous life proofing.

Sort of like how you weather- proof your house. I will also add not as an excuse because honestly if I really wanted to, I could have chosen to find other means necessary to do so. During lock down I became isolated from not only the opportunity to travel home but also not able to participate in ceremony. The substance that fed my Soul. I was finding places to rent that did not allow me to smudge in them.

There went that luxury well. Many years before in a sweat lodge Uncle shared with us." What if there comes a time where there is no more sweat lodge, no more smudge, no more outside medicine, ceremony.

Do you have it within you to go to that place of zero.to empty the mind this way, letting go of pretending, of ego, of the stories we tell ourselves and others." I guess the answer to that had come.

If I was to be honest about where I thought I was at, I'd say I was only getting enough of a grade to advance to the bottom of the next class. During my last visit I was staying with my Sundance brother and his wife, my adopted sister from Mt Currie that now lived in Burnaby. She worked for a large grocery chain and told me told me that one of the stores was looking for a Temporary Vitamins Manager at another location. This was right up my alley, so I dropped a resume off and applied on their career site. Leaving the result up to Creator.

I decided that if I got the job that meant my decision to move back was the way to go. Well, I got the job. Coincidentally I also found a reasonable room to rent within a 10-minute drive from work. All this came together within a month which was amazing despite evolving right at the beginning of the now infamous pandemic. I felt despite the challenges, uncertainty, and chaos swirling around the world, if I donned the attitude of head down ass up work ethic and pushed my way along, I could still envision myself living the dream. I felt like this was how I was going to spend the remaining working years ahead.

That was until in January of 2022. When I sustained the afore mentioned back injury. This time to my lower back. It dropped me to the floor sending me to the hospital, which followed by the next year and a half recovering. It involved the usual physiotherapy, a 7-week Pain management program followed by Aqua therapy that I continued my own.

I was enrolled in a 4 month online retraining program covering all the basic aspects of Office worker. All covered by the government. I have heard so many stories from individuals and in previous years have had nothing but problematic incidents with them, but I must say this time every step of my experience with them I received nothing but support, compassion, and care.

During this time my job ended, so despite having been educated as a Natural Health Practitioner and practising for 18 years, at the age of 62 it took 37 resumes' submitted in 6 weeks to FINALLY land back into the work force in what I thought was for sure this time, my forever most perfectly suited job in July 2023.

Teachings from Uncle ....

Winter Solstice. A truly sacred time to participate in long standing rituals that can create an opportunity to practise whatever Ceremony that further deepens our, dare say the word, Faith. Not just the whole believing in things unseen, but with it this concept that involves a degree of trust and willingness to know deep within.

The knowing which occurs not in the mind but as a sense vibrating throughout the body which assures us the desired result will in fact happen beyond any doubt. In the Sundance way the Preparation for the next years annual Ceremony starts the day after Sundance is over and continuing throughout the full year ahead.

Through the year Ceremonies within Ceremonies at Auspicious times are entered. Fasting for the 4 days during Thanksgiving and Easter is one of these preparations. Not the I won't eat carbs or sugars kind of fasting.

During this time, we focus on the clearing away or letting go if you will, any mental, emotional, Spiritual, baggage that could hold us back from being completely present and connected to Source during the Sundance. This is in the hopes of achieving clarity and understanding of the path we have chosen. Its easy to be spiritual with a bag of Doritos and the remote control in front of your favorite show but take away all means of security and comfort can you, do you have what it takes to go in? Sundance is held as close to Summer Solstice as possible.

During the year, we gather all we needed to participate in this 4-day way of Prayer or as the Sundance Chief said, "a celebration of life and welcoming the new year! Preparation for the next year starts the day after we have finished the Sundance." From the gathering of all our camping gear to the ceremonial clothing and accessories we will wear. There are various teachings and protocols in honouring the Winter Solstice depending on the Territory, culture, and beliefs. During my second year Uncle shared one of his with me that explained the reasoning behind a specific task, ritual if you will for the shortest day of the year. The making of our Prayer flags from certain colors of broad cloth and tobacco. These would then be offered up and tied to what we referred to as the Tree of life.

Every year the searching of this Tree that would be offering itself up was sought out through a prayerful vision before being ceremoniously taken down by the male dancers taking turns with an axe. It was then escorted by all the dancers, leaders, supporters, and all other participants back to the Sundance grounds and raised in the middle of the arbor where we the dancers would spend the next 4 days. I had my 4 colours of prints, smudge, and tobacco for this ritual, and I set them aside on my Altar. off to sweat lodge I went.

I was excited because this cleansing was to be very special to honour the Winter Solstice. Uncle started talking about the days that would follow this day of and how with the daylight lengthening, this light that came from Source, the sun, would give strength to what we paid attention to daily.

In the Old ways on this day the prayer flags and all the items we would need such as the Pipe tobacco, smudge we would use for the 4 days, piercing feathers if that was part of our commitment amongst other items was made into a sacred bundle. Every day after, this bundle would be prayed with until Ceremony time.

This way of looking after our prayers was not only to help us stay connected to the Ceremony but to the prayers themselves from within. As the days grew longer the Suns energy, Creators strength that was called upon to solidify our faith, all that was being put out into the Spirit realm became a part of us. Every day I smudged it, recommitted my heart, my spirit to the way of life I had chosen contained partially in this Bundle.

Come Tree Day that year as I opened the bundle to offer the flags to the Tree of Life, I felt this incredible surge of strength, clarity, a knowing of sorts that they would be answered in the best way possible and that my small part in this time was exactly as it was supposed to be. I had goosebumps all over.

There was such a feeling of joy, of deep heart sacredness within that from then on this was how I prepared. Uncle has been with his ancestors for a time now.

I really can miss him…

If the teaching fits….

After a few proverbial kicks at the cat, I have managed to sober up for what so far has been 33 years of continuous clean time. Even with so much one day at a times behind me, I have spent more moments than deemed necessary living in the dilapidated neighbourhood called my mind. Rejecting the very place that my heart had been searching to restore. I became very good at avoidance, at projecting my internal world was in good standing by focusing on helping others.

This denial manifested showing itself quite clearly during my Sundance days. I would spend the year prepping making sure I had everything. Not just for myself but also for the other women dancers and helpers. Things like extra prints for the tree if needed. Safety pins for the women's dresses.

Piercing feathers, extra smudge, etc. this way of "helping" I later learned was because even though I was of the belief that creator wanted me there, I wasn't sure the Humans felt the same way. As a result of some of their Trauma, having someone being involved in their sacred ways of healing that was non-indigenous was triggering for some.
It took me awhile to understand that Ceremony no matter the kind is comprised of individuals that are all on a healing path in some degree or another and as such they are like me in that our humanness will reveal those aspects, we have come to honestly look at and make the decision to either move forward or attempt to put these wounds back in the box.

I felt that if I made myself indispensable then they wouldn't kick me out of the space that my spirit felt was where I belonged. I spent 14 years walking this path. There came a time however when it didn't matter how I I tried to get to the next Sundance, roadblocks kept coming up that prevented the follow through. I was finally told by a wise one that this was because my time involved in this way was done. That I had fulfilled and learned what was meant to be. It was interesting how these words coincided with the message shared by the Sundance Chief years before.

He had told me "Many people will spend their lives deeply involved in the Sundance while others it is only a part of their journey through life." I have since come to learn that although I would spend the year preparing for Sundance, Sundance prepared me for life.

The Sundance arbor was a structured circle with openings across from each other in 4 directions. At sunrise we would line up and enter the arbour from the east gate. As the drums and singers would begin, we would collectively direct our focus in our own individual way of prayer.

With no time frame scheduled we danced clockwise in the circle stopping at each direction to dance and pray there until we were at the south gate. If I was to hazard a guess this generally took about 2-3 hours maybe longer? By the time we would reach this gate you could see the exhaustion in all of us.

We had given it our all to the commitment of this what we called a round, but it was not over until the drums and singing stopped. Only then could we make our way out of the arbour to go rest. Many times, outside of Sundance in everyday life, I would be in that place of the mind, body and spirit that just couldn't do another step, endure one more second of challenge, nor withstand the brunt of yet another what would be seen later as a teachable moment. In these instances, sometimes I had the wherefore all to equate what was going on presently and muster up the means needed to come out the other side, I would remind myself I was at the South gate.

It wouldn't be long until I could rest. So, it has been the way of this present Cancer experience. This procedure of the dance was done up to 7-8 times in a day, every day for a 4-day period. During the whole time there was no consumption of food or water by the dancers.

The public, which was those that supported outside the Arbor did and we were always very grateful. For they kept us in their thought and prayers as they ate to "feed" us, our spirits as well. This way of connection was very real. I can attest to that.

After my fourth year I was unable to go over to Alberta at thanksgiving to help the fasters but right from the very first day of their fast I started craving bacon so badly that I finally had make my way to the grocery store where I picked up 2 packages.

Over the next 3 days cooked it up and ate it. On the 4th day the intense cravings stopped just as suddenly as they had started. I knew it had to have been someone fasting over there just wishing for it.

A few days later I was talking on the phone with one of my Sundance sisters and told her my experience. She revealed that a couple of the women had gone on their moon time and so set their tents up away from everyone else's over by the main house on the grounds and they could smell bacon cooking every morning coming from the house.

Apparently, whoever was staying there was making it as part of the breakfast for the Sundance chief who lived there! Every time I would head over to fast my youngest would tell me "I'll eat and drink for you Mom" and you know, during those times I never ever had an issue with hunger or thirst.

As life has continued, the knowing that someone cares deeply for me enough to support my journeys in a way that they understand has contributed to my belief I will come out the other side in a good way regardless the circumstances.

Working through the fear…

I have rarely ever had a fear of traveling, moving to new places, cities, provinces, trying new things, jobs on my own. Partly because I thought I was tough. But also, because it just never really occurred to me that anything bad was going to happen "out there" in places I was unfamiliar with.

I had been through so much already mentally emotional physically and spiritually in my everyday life that I saw the unknown as opportunities for adventure and change. After what was a very busy and profitable winter in the Spa in 2014, I decided to travel to Peru. I toured some of the more notable places like the city of Nazca to fly over the legendary archaeological site containing the Nazca lines. Got thrown off a cliff (yes on purpose) in a tandem paragliding episode in Lima.

Let me tell you, NOW that was a holy moly moment!! In lima right on the coastline there are these huge cliffs accessible by driving right up to them from the city. I needed to do this.

This trip was a journey of being committed to trying new things, things that scared the bee gees out of me. and tandem paragliding was on that list. The whole having nothing to set the feet on with reaching heights that turned full scale vehicles into tiny spots moving about below. It was sticky and humid yet hot and sunny out if that makes any sense. I could hear the waves crashing on the beach below. Seemed to take forever to get strapped in securing the fate of me to that of my guide. The longer it took the more my nerves were shaking me up.

At what seemed like the last minute I was just about to call it off, the fellow that had tethered us together had other plans and in one quick motion suddenly grabbed our combined harness and began running, propelling us towards the edge of the cliff.

With one fell swoop I was instantly thrashing my feet in the air trying to find something solid to walk on. I could hear this screaming at the top of the lungs like a little schoolgirl. Turns out it was me. Didn't know I had that kind of volume.

Once I realized I was safe gliding about, I was able to hear my guides voice reassuring me I was ok. He started telling me all about the view, encouraging me to just sit back into the harness and allow him to steer the parachute. For what seemed like a very long time we soared up and down the coastline. What an experience! Before we turned around to head back, we passed by some 30 floor heavily windowed towers, and it was so cool seeing our reflection in them. Just like the movies!! Towards the end I was chatting it up laughing and wishing we could go forever. Unfortunately, it did have to come to an end and as we headed towards the base preparing to land, I saw another tandem pair being hurled towards its edge.

The passenger a very large burly man who to my chagrin, was emitting that same little schoolgirl wail!! Ha! Didn't feel so bad now about my reaction after all. Other than heights the biggest fear I had was open waters. Especially if I couldn't see the bottom. So of course, the next activity was to take a surfing lesson. By the end of the day however, even though I was able to stand erect for 6 seconds, I had decided that I would never been doing that again. I learned just because we try something whether we fail or succeed at it, doesn't mean we have to commit fully and unconditionally to the continued participation in it for the rest of our lives. I mean, to whom and what are we trying to prove.

Believe it or not We can hold up our hand and say "Nah, I'm good. Thanks though" and keep on moving. With the adventures in Peru my trust in the Universe became almost like a forced trust in other human beings. Not a practise I regularly invoked. In my mind all the pain and suffering throughout my life had been human caused. I decided long ago, perhaps before I had even realized on a conscious level that trusting no one would probably get me a lot further without the inevitable scarring outcome of the experience.

 Up to this point I had lived my life in such a way that I could not see any point of reference that showed me otherwise. That doesn't mean there weren't any, it just means I didn't "see" them. I find it interesting that so many simple daily tasks, habits become so much more than just that when applying them to the daily routine in a place that is not home, more so in another town, city, or foreign country.

These tasks gain a whole new life and sometimes reverence of their own. Maybe that's why we can assume the only way to become enlightened or have that most sought-after Spiritual experience is to do so away from the everyday.

Could be a plausible explanation as to why every time my life seemed to be in another spiral downwards, I'd suddenly feel the intense urge to move. To another apartment, another city or Province. This illusion of reclaiming my sanity was guaranteed to be followed by a brief period of what I call the honeymoon stage. Where life was good again. No tragedies, no toxic workplaces, no daily incidents that created pain. The only trouble with this methodology was that everywhere I went; I took me with me.

Full circle....

Before I made the decision to embark on this Peruvian path of healing, or should I say before it was shown to me that it was already in the works by Spirit. I was planning on a trip to an Ashram in India. However, it was shared by a trusted friend that it was not the time to go, especially since I wanted to travel by myself as usual. It would not be safe. Another time in the future perhaps.

As soon as I decided ok, the doors opened up out of what seemed like nowhere for what was to be one of the most authentic, experience I have been blessed with. People, all the travel plans, where I would stay on each leg of the trip, even the Shipibo Maestra revealed and set themselves in place.

I made my way South to Cusco where from here I took the bus to the city of Machu Picchu at the mountain base of the Lost City of the Incas as it is commonly referred to.

Before I had left my home, I knew I needed to offer up the sacred Chanunpa in prayer for the region and its people. Once I started the climb up the ridge to the ruins I immediately understood why. There was a constant flurry of excitement and chatter amongst the many tourists from all over the world but beyond that excitement my heart felt heavy. The energy of the majestic overgrown remains of a time long ago was empty.

It felt like my spirit does when I have stayed too long in a place where interactions with other humans seems to have sucked the life force out of me and I'm left feeling drained. This ancient Being in the form of the lost city felt so exhausted. The energy was such I wanted to curl up and sleep. This was the vibration Mother Earth in this place was emitting. She invoked an image of a mother who has given all her moments of the day to her unyielding children constantly tugging at her leg demanding.

The mothers face showing the weariness but her eyes shining through it with the unconditional love a mother can have for her child regardless of circumstance. The many years of humans rolling over the crest into her village subconsciously dumping unconsciously all their pain and suffering.

Filling their souls cup back up with the purity of what she offered without conditions. This was not why I had come. I had no intention of dumping. I only wanted to give. I followed the crowds oohing and aahing at the magnificence of the culture that once made this place their home until I came to the top of the ridge.

On a patch of greenery by the shell of a stone building I took a seat and opened the bundle, filling the Pipe and digging deep within for the prayers that were asking to be heard. I had let the gatekeepers at the start of the trail know what I had wanted to do, and they understood.

Giving me their permission as well as the protocols that no fires even if it was a smudge or the Pipe to be lit. A kind one however told me once I was done praying, I could head down the back side off trail into the treed area to complete the ceremony releasing the prayers by smoking it. It was an honor indeed.

My heart felt full, peaceful, in gratitude that at some point previous I had set aside my ego and all about me issues to hear Creator for a moment in time to pray not for myself but for that past, present, and yet to come just as the ones who came before me had done for me. This was Purposefulness.... The next adventure propelled me into the Amazon via the Amazon River which flowed right past the village of San Francisco where I spent 10 days in a yurt with a Shipibo Family sharing their Ancestral ways of the Ayahuasca medicine.

The first night sitting with Maestra Justina whom I originally met up with in Lima before we flew to Pucallpa and taking the river journey. I was excited, nervous yet holding strong in the belief that this time with the Medicine was exactly where I was supposed to be. I managed to swallow the putrid raw dark brown liquid and waited. I had previously on a few occasions with the Peyote before, so my mind was expecting a similar session with Source. Yes and no. It wasn't too long of before I was on my back, my heart filling with this sensation so pure and blissful I could only rationalize it to be love. "I love you chickens' I said in response to their days end acknowledgements. "I love you puppy dog"

I laughed thinking maybe the puppy and the chickens were having a back n forth banter. Then I was gone or should I say my Spirit was gone, left my body and headed towards the vast darkened skies of the night.

The stars had shaped themselves into a heart and I was determined to go there.... It was a short trip. I was sent back to my body to allow the Medicine to work with me until the early hours of the morning.

The second night, took the drink, laid myself down and off I went again. This time leaving my body for the Eye of God that shone brightly in the night sky. Again, back to the body I was sent. The wonderful part of working with the Medicine is that I could talk to it as I would to an old friend sitting beside me. I was confused. These last 2 beginnings of ceremony were so profound and beautiful why was I not allowed to stay there? She answered quickly with compassion" You need to be in your body because this is where the basic structure of the work needs to be done. By leaving you are avoiding." My body became clammy, my heart pounding seemingly trying to exit my chest by any means possible. I recognized this familiar sensation instantly.

This was fear! it had suddenly washed over and through me in the most powerful way I had not experienced in a very long time. As if on cue Maestra Justina soothing voice carrying the Icaros was cradling my fear. Even though I knew she was seated across the yurt with the 3 other Shamans, it was like she was singing right into my right ear. Her voice was calming enough to allow me to travel for the first time in a while the complete journey from my head to my heart. I'd had moments similar but not as intense as this during Sundance and other ceremonies for a short time. But then it would be back up to the head to retreat.

The place in which I was way too ready to hang out regardless of the blatant evidence that this "comfortable" zone that was my mind did not have my best interests at heart. I like to say my heads like a bad neighbourhood, don't go there alone. A wise one said once "if you're going upstairs, take a friend!" The next two nights of Ceremony were just as powerful in their own ways. It was like the first night addressed the mental.

At one point during that night the Medicine worked tirelessly on my head and face. It felt like She was restructuring, pulling every cell apart, then with a fine baby haired paint brush, gently whisked away the trauma of the past that I had inadvertently stored in these cellular spaces to deal with at another time before lovingly put them back into their perspective place. During night 2 She continued down my body right to my feet stopping at each physical injury I had sustained over the course of my time.

The 3rd night, I cried, oh how I cried. From the very depths of little Heidis abandoned heart. As the sunlight made its way through the jungle treetops that rose high above the Yurt on the 4th morning, my willingness to expose and offer up that most vulnerable sacred aspect of who I was as a Soul sister to the medicine of the Songs let itself be known. I was ready.

These methodic rhythms of the Shipibo ways were now being sung not only by the 4 Shamans but also a young man who was a nephew to one of them sitting directly across from me in the yurt.

While he transcended through the lineage of ancestral medicine, I finally sat up feeling strong and whole.

My body started to sway, sway in a way not unlike that of a Cobra poised to hypnotize their prey. I opened my eyes at one point and the young man's physicality had been replaced with yes, a majestic cobra whose iridescent metallic blue veil opened, spanning far and wide.

I instinctively knew this was HER, her ancient eyes held strong on me a gaze that said neither disappointment nor pleasure. just a knowing, an understanding.

I felt heard! When I shared through an interpreter to Maestra Justina that morning's closure, she said' Yes, the Medicine was letting me know it was a good journey. That the circle of my healing time with Her was done." By the time the Amazon nights of healing sessions were over, it felt like all 4 aspects of my Medicine wheel had been tended to in a most sacred, ancient way that finally allowed them to connect with each other in a way that probably hadn't been since before my conception.

Back home I was sharing my trip experiences and what I thought/felt I'd learned, I was told; "This is good. It's important to experience other cultures, their ways, their medicine. Just remember if you were meant to practise those ways as a way of life you would have been born there. But you weren't, these are your ways" He was referring to the way of life, the walking of the Red Road that I had 15 years ago by this time completely welcomed and implemented into my life.

From the time I stepped onto it even though I was not indigenous it felt like this was the practise of a lineage behind me and I belonged. It was my true path. With his words, words I trusted wholly as in all the words he had ever shared with me, I felt not only accepted 100% but my Spirit, that space within me that seemed 100 miles away from my body was home. Back in. I felt complete.

Voices from beyond….

I believe all my life or at least as far back in my time here, I have had a somewhat connection to those on the other side of the veil. I remember being around 5 or 6 when I found a robin laying in the corner by the fence in our backyard. It was so still. The concept of death wasn't yet in my awareness at that age. I had been so far shielded. Even when our dog Papoose was no longer with us, I assumed she was on a farm somewhere.

My child mind or was it my own Spirit was telling me I had to do something. That I was meant to do something. I gently picked it up, cradling it in the palms of my tiny hands and while looking down on it I thought it was sleeping. Like sleeping beauty in the story. What woke her up? A kiss. A kiss from someone who cared for her.

Well, I cared for this robin. I raised the quiet body up to my lips, leaning in for the life saving kiss that would bring its spirit back with a fluttering of wings before it would fly away home. That was not the case.

She was indeed already across into the other realm. I don't remember what happened after that moment or where it went but I do know I ended up in the bathroom being force fed a bar of soap to remove any diseases this feathered friend might have inadvertently transferred to me. I was very confused. I thought that what I did was an obvious act of what one was supposed to do in that situation! Our Past-Ons show up for many reasons they say. They present themselves in a way that we intuitively understand.

Before I got clean and sober, different experiences happened to make me pause but I didn't equate them to this phenomenon. Having said that, it doesn't mean there weren't any that I can put to paper right now. Maybe as I continue to write they will show themselves…. Not long after deciding to get it together however is a whole other story! The boys and I were living in a four-plex in Vernon.

I loved this split-level unit where the bedrooms and full bathroom were on the second floor. I always felt, especially when I was alone, that I wasn't if you know what I mean. It was like if I turned around abruptly, I would catch a glimpse of whoever was standing there, just watching. They say when you sober up there is only one thing you need to change, and that's everything. Well, I truly tried but one thing I wasn't letting go of was my music. I felt like it was all I had left other than my boys from my previous life that was good.

One of my most favorite musicians was Janis Joplin. I loved her so much that on my home landline answering machine. I used her song Mercedes Benz as the voice message. So, one day I'm in the kitchen prepping supper when suddenly without the phone ringing to activate the voice message, Janise's song started playing on the machine. I went over to it thinking well that's weird and tried to shut if off. It wouldn't, it would just rewind then start again.

This was freaking me out. It did this 4 times. Each time when I couldn't get it to stop, I unplugged the machine from the wall, waited a few minutes then plugged it back in. Back to cooking I go when I'll be dammed if it doesn't happen again. I tried pressing al the buttons once more thinking it would help. Nope. Finally, I just said with a voice like I was chastising one of my kids" Janis! will you stop it! "And she did…….

Another time a few months later me and the boys and my what was to be 2nd husband were all in the living room can't remember the whys of it but there we were when my disposable camera that I had sitting on top of the fridge started initiating the flash all by itself. When I went in to retrieve it, it stopped. Never did figure out who that was.

In 2015 I was camped out for a month in one of Natures most pristine spots just down the road from Mt Currie. My designated camp site was not just perfectly flat, which can be very hard to find to pitch the tent or level the RV, it was surrounded by these majestic Douglas fir trees systematically anchored with their roots just off a large flowing creek. Here someone had taken the time to create a mini pool surrounded by boulders and the like.

This became my freshen me up spot as I was part of the recycling clean-up crew from the Pemberton music festival event that occurred for the second season. It generally took place at the beginning of summer.

Those 10-hour days of being emersed in the sticky stench of the job left a film upon my persons that only the earths pure bathwater could remove. During my stay so much happened, bears came through destroying campsites, windstorms blew their cleansing breath downing trees left and right, cougars roamed through looking for easy prey. All this happened around me but not once affected my site, or me.

When I was tearing down and packing up at the end of my stay it was shown why. It was time to tear everything down and head out. I hadn't realized how comfy I had made my self until it took several trips back and forth to the car to get the process done.

With the tent finally empty I got out my handy dandy dollar store little hand broom and dustpan and swept the inside out. As I stepped out of the doorway one last time to empty the pan something caught my eye on the ground right in front of the door. I had crossed over that threshold hundreds of times in my stay and never saw this before. I bent to pick it up and started to cry. It was a robin's egg blue plastic guitar pick. I knew instantly why my stay had been incident free. You see my ex-husbands favorite color was robins egg blue and he played lead guitar.

This memento was his way of letting me know he had been there watching over, protecting me this whole time. I cleaned off the pick and later gave it to his son sharing the story of how it came about.

Every time I think of him my heart feels the love which I continue to carry these many years. I still shed tears on occasion when I think of some of those precious times together. These episodes started happening around the time people that walked a sacred path on the Red Road, were being put or showing up however you see it, into my life This spiritual path is called that as the name and its cultural practices originated with the Indigenous Peoples.

An Elder had said the road can seem wide in the beginning allowing for the humanness and corrections to the understandings of the ways but as time goes on it becomes quite narrow the further you walk along it. I was by now having lengthy in-depth sharing with a couple of old timers in the program that I sobered with. The topics of these conversations ranged from how we were related to all living things. the ways to honor our Past Ons, the Creator, the sweat lodge and later with other teachers outside the program, plant medicine and their spirits.

The first time I was ever in a sweat lodge, despite my eagerness to participate I was overwhelmed with anxiety and fear. The minute the door made of many blankets slid down to engulf us in darkness with only the glow of the Heated grandfathers in the center, I panicked. I couldn't breathe. Every fibre of my being needed to get out and get out now.

I practically ran over the Grandfathers calling out "all my relations ". Before the door was even halfway opened, I was on the other side of it gasping in the fresh air. I was so disappointed in myself. I felt I had let the person who was kind enough to bring me into this most sacred circle down. He wasn't upset though. He just told me everything happened the way it was supposed to and that I needed to strengthen my faith.

Over the next couple of years, I attended two more and the same thing happened. I couldn't get past the first few minutes once that door was closed. If it was open though, I was perfectly fine. I beat myself up for quite awhile that I didn't have enough faith. I ran with the perception of someone else's opinion as to what the reasoning behind it all was. It wasn't until I found myself with my husband having the exact same inner experience while we were bivouacked in the snow on a glacier just below the peak of Mt Sir Donald in the Revelstoke Pass.

We were in the tiniest of tents that barely fit us both. It suddenly dawned on me that it wasn't a lack of faith. I wasn't doing or wasn't something wrong, I was claustrophobic for crying out loud!

Since we couldn't just pack up and leave to go down, my poor husband had to spend the night with the door of the tent opened so when I would periodically open my eyes, to see the moons glow off the false face of Sir Donald peak lighting up the sky as if dusk was never going to end.

Not long after this realization I took the desire and willingness to let go of this claustrophobia into the healing sweat lodge giving up to the Spirit helpers.

It came from the very first place I was meant to be cared for and protected before coming into this world. The womb was a very scary place.
Filled with fear, anger and generational trauma being fed to me though the cord to my mother.
I can say from the healing through this I have not experienced that issue again. I will say that the spiritual tools I have adapted into my life over time work as well today as they did in the beginning. Among the many words in my heart that have been placed there is the Blackfoot term Iikaakimaat I learned in Ceremony many years ago which means "try hard, keep going."

Making the most of it....

What's that phrase?" pain is inevitable, but suffering is optional." One of the benefits of not taking others' opinions on as your own personal truth regardless of who it is that's sharing, is you can save yourself a whole lot of needless suffering, self doubt, and potentially made-up issues that you now must dig through to heal from. If I have been in a place of willingness at some time or another to continue to heal, grow and learn and have been asking for the support of the Universe, then doesn't it stand to reason that my experiences have been the result of these thoughts wishes and demands.

I feel like the Universe does not operate on the good or bad scale; it operates on giving us what we ask for to fulfill the task. As a result of this belief, I have learned to be more specific with my requests. I get this visual of the Universe doling out the experiences mumbling to themselves "now I think this is what she meant" while trying to match it up. During the dark challenging moments is the perfect time when I need to say" thank you Universe ...thank you for hearing me and supporting me."

But I also need to acknowledge and take responsibility for how I communicated the asking for help or the way in which I attempted to manifest a desired outcome. The blame game serves no purpose but results only in the perpetual illusion that somehow, I am the victim. Which was exactly how I thought during some of my dysfunctional days. I used to say "If you had a husband like mine, you'd drink too. Or everyone at work is an idiot and I just can't with them. The landlord just doesn't understand and is greedy. Everyone hates me." Blah blah blah.

The only purpose I now feel in looking at others and their part in my suffering is to use them as the proverbial mirror that will tell me truthfully where I am at any given moment in my mind, heart, and spirit. I can then choose to move forward in my journey. Or not. Easier said then done I might add. I usually can come to these insights after (sometimes long after) the pain and suffering is over. I think every experience we have, yes, we are the center player in it, but once it is over it is up to me to be able to let it go in the sense that it has now become a source of support or knowledge for another down the road. It is no longer about me even though it remains as part of my story. Each time a portion is brought to light in a share, my only hope and desire is that it comes from a place of non-attachment.

One of my childhood dreams for when I grew old enough was to have this big old farm with many acres. It would be filled with all the cats and dogs that ended up in the SPCA. There would be little homes on the land for injured animals I rescued. I needed to feel needed.

In my early teens our class had been using these adorable little albino mice to perform nutritional tests in science class and when we were done, they had to go back to the University where they became their snakes' meals. I was horrified so home the one I was working with came! I named it Seymour. He could fit up to 16 shelled sunflower seeds in the sides of its mouth.

There was a succession of rescues. Salamanders that I had to feed by hand live daddy long legged spiders I pulled off the skirting of the trailer, a mangy putrid smelling cat that was in the neighbourhood which I brought in, bathed, and fed for a few days before I had to let it go. Spending time with creatures that didn't seem to mind my attention fed my wounded soul. As I got older my attention shifted from animals to other neglected or wounded humans.

One can say I was wholly attached to the idea that my personal worth was based on how much I gave to others while sacrificing my own needs and wants. That is up until around 2011 when everything became way too much.

All the dysfunction in relationships both professional and personal that I was the common denominator in became so great, I finally conceded to my inner most self that it would be in my best interests to get marching myself into a Cognitive trauma Therapist. I threw my hands in the air and announced how absolutely, unequivocally that I was DONE. Done with the pain. Done with the suffering, so done with what seemed like a repetition of experiences with slight differences. I was 100 % willing to do whatever it took to break the cycle. Time is fleeting. Moments ever so precious. These thoughts have proven themselves to be true on so many levels.

Time that a dragonfly will unselfishly give to you. So, when it presents itself in your path, take heed. For their life span is so short. An adult life is approximately six months. A blink of an eye really. When they are using some of that to grace you with their presence, give gratitude. This is the teaching they bring. In remembering this when I came across one in the middle of the bike path on a hike I was doing, my heart immediately pushed me forward to move it somewhere safer. It held no fear as it crawled onto my outstretched finger.

As I attempted to place it gently on a tree leaf it kept crawling backwards to stay on my finger. The trust it held in me was so moving I almost cried but instead I just kept telling it "Thank you" Thank you for choosing me in this moment that I do not need to analyze. Since that time, it has on more than one occasion been enough to just say "Thank you" as moments appear in my life.

My life had to this point made great strides in many areas. I had traveled internationally, held unique employment, even received further education to become a Certified Natural Health Practitioner.

But there was in the background a feeling that something was missing, something I wasn't catching on to that led me to this healing time with someone I could trust with my bare soul. She saved me from crashing myself into the wall head on. Today I live in a suburban area where what started with 2 crows is now a murder of 5 or 6. Is that a murder? I am not sure how many constitutes one. There are 2 black squirrels and one grey and as of late a momma raccoon and her welp from last year that visit me on the regular.

They get their treats, comfort me with their presence before they are off to where or whomever else is on their list to frequent. Although I feed them and make sure they have fresh water, especially when its hot out, our relationships are not coming from this illusion that I am helping them. In fact, it's quite the opposite. Just the way their timely appearances in my life these last couple years have organically happened, tells me they showed up to help and support me. The loneliness of the pandemic, Isolation while recovering from injuries and most recent losing my job 3 weeks before I was to undergo a successful cancer removal surgery.

This has been the hardest, absolute hardest time of my days here. with them being here checking in/up on me, pretending to need me kept me physically moving about. Has encouraged me to find joy in the watching of their little quirks, chatting with them like I would a person in my presence then sharing in text or on the old FB (Facebook). Between them and the gift of living in the most perfect quiet home with an incredibly affordable rent.

 A secluded back yard surrounded by not only beautiful seasonal flowering plants but two grandmother cedars that must be at least 3 stories tall for me to tend to. I'll be the first to say the good Creator sure knows His stuff. The opportunity to be in this space currently is no coincidence. A scenario set for what is now the deepest level of healing of mind body and spirit that I have yet gone through.

◆◆◆

Spontaneous healing...

Last spring after 87 years on this earth my mom decided it was time to go. In July my older sister in her travels from saskatoon brought to my home her ashes. My mom's wish was to join her mom in going to the ocean. My niece and I were going to honor that. I'd already came into Grandmas ashes not long before Mom showed up. Then I was diagnosed with stage 3 Ovarian Cancer. Mom and Grandmas final journey would have to wait...

March of 2024 I was finally able to honour her wishes and so with a sorrowful heart I took the first steps in truly letting go unconditionally with love, forgiveness and some peace.

As I look back, touching on what seems to be the most prevalent events or time frames of challenges, teachings gained, lessons learned, I realize that every single experience I've had have been levels of preparation to get through and be successful through this latest life event. I have consequently reviewed some of the notes mentally taken from those times more than once I'll say.

On a lighter note, one such experience was when I was just a littler girl maybe 4 or 5? while I am visiting my grandparents in Pointe Gatineau Quebec, I found myself one day on my grandpa's lap looking amazed at how shiny his head was from no hair. In my childlike innocence I told him "One day I want a haircut just like your grandpa".

Recently now after the second chemo treatment the hair was starting to come out in clumps, so off I went to my go to style gal, and she honoured me with that wish 57 years later!! I will admit it felt kind of neat and at the same time so freeing. There is so much ego attached to our hair. Thinking about my mom, I know we were never able to have a healthy relationship and I had mostly come to terms with that long ago. I grieved for many years while she was here. The grief that rises occasionally now is the loss of someone that I have loved and cared about is no longer here, but also sad for her, the losses she incurred because of her decisions and actions.

Yet I am grateful. For she has been here in spirit since the summer and I have felt all that she can emanate now that she no longer carries the limitations of being in this world, this realm. Thanks mom these few months have been the scariest I have lived yet, and I have felt your love and support. How do I know she has been here? The same way I knew when Grandma "visited "a few months after she had crossed over.

It happened 5 or 6 times over a two-month period. I would be in a deep sleep and suddenly be awakened by a voice that I recognized as Grandmas whispering in my left ear my name." HEIDI". It was right around the time I was going to have a partial hysterectomy. Although it was meant to heal, it felt so invasive which left me feeling violated.

Back to most recent, the night I was brought home from the intensive thorough but successful cancer surgery, I was awakened during the night with two gentle compressions through the quilt on my right leg just above my ankle. They were the kind one would administer to someone you cared about to reassure them that they were ok and were being looked after.

My heart knew it was mom. I believe part of our medicine wheel of life is comprised of Emotional, Spiritual, Physical, and mental. Any time we have an imbalance in any one area because of traumatic events or lack of completion in an experience, we store the wound somewhere in our body.

When it stays stored or hidden away for long enough, the emotional, mental, or spiritual wound will manifest itself into a physical illness or dis-ease if you will. It is what is called the last cry for help and resolution, closure.

Back to the beginning....

Right from the moment on the phone with my doctor when he was sharing the results of the CT scan with contrast, even though I was shocked, upset, from then through this whole time I have never felt like this was going to be the experience that was going to end my life. However, I knew this was going to be one hell of a challenging time unlike any other I had gone through up till now.

One of the first things I did after I let the diagnosis sit for a few days, had a couple cries, then stocked up on all the various natural supplements for immune building and Anti-oxidative components. Made appointments for Acupuncture, Vibrational sound healing sessions. I will say have been the best complimentary modalities alongside Chemo for side affects.

As a second level Reiki Practitioner I began a regular regime of Self applications working with this wondrous Life Force Energy. Then I went inward. Inward to the place of knowing.

I went back, all the way back. I had to. For this was the start. Back to the beginning of being brought into this world. I slowly made my way though my life stopping at various specific events. I Reviewed some of what felt like the most tragic. I also viewed the times of triumph, the times of growth in my Spirit, the subtle changes in my heart and mind. It didn't take long for me to put together the reasoning behind why this visitor showed up.

Although this would logically seem to be a good spot to insert an experience that left its scars, I find when calling upon them in my mind there doesn't feel the need. Is it because I have healed for the most part?

I am not sure if it's because I would rather forget, or if it is because if I lay these most vulnerable painful moments before you that you will see me differently. That you, as I did once, assume that these occurrences were who I was, not just what I went through.

That you will move from no longer my champion of sorts but into a place of judgement on the poor choices I and those around me made that created the pain.

I also realize that in the constant regurgitation also known as analysis paralysis, of some moments in my life I re-create an attachment once again to them. In this attachment I lose the freedom I have gained from healing. Yes, some reflection is important, if it serves a purposefulness without defining a whole other characterization of who I am. Not to say these events will never be shared again, only that they will when they are called upon to support another in understanding the how's and what's they are going through. To share for the benefit of relatability.

Of not feeling alone. For the one seeking connection. I know during my times of connection; the most successful growth came from being able to relate to someone who had been through what I had. Having said that what follows is I feel an insight to the visitor's appearance. From as far back as I can remember in my childhood and early teens, I was repeatedly denied the opportunity and support to develop and live in the female aspects of who I was in the most authentic way.

I was told I was hated because I wasn't a boy when I was born by my mother at a very young age. After time in therapy as an adult I understood where her anger was coming from. Her trauma came from a father whose belief was that a woman's sole purpose was to sire sons and he was given all daughters. He treated not only them but my grandma as insignificant and withheld his love and acceptance from them. I feel that she was hoping if she had a grandson to present to him, she would receive this.

The purity of my female essence was violated with a violence and cruelty on more than one occasion that further re-enforced the message that what was supposed to be the most sacred aspect of me was not... I also know that with this aspect of being female and how it translated into bringing forth life came the struggles to develop long lasting relationships with these gifts I call my sons. Although two have come around there is one who has chosen to deny me the option of being called his mother.

I understand and respect his choice while coming to terms with this. He has not been heard from by anyone in the family for a few years. As a result, I have not been able to share in the most genuine way my sorrow for all I put him through. I have yet not been able to complete the circle with him and so my journey in honouring myself as a life giver does not feel warranted. I use the word visitor in referring to the Cancer because right from the start I was not going to form any attachment to it.

I decided to choose the language I used around it to reflect that. I understood that by using the words or thoughts that said, 'I have", it creates a bond if you will. The reality is that any time I am attached to something or someone whether be good or bad for my wellbeing, it becomes a most difficult challenge that creates much suffering when I make the decision to let go. One of my character defects is that in the process of the letting go whatever "it" is, creates a whole ordeal that can become a long and arduous, bloody fight leaving me scarred and battered.

The decision to let go for me at any time has been either the result of fearing I was losing something, someone that completed me, or verified my worthiness. I remember a couple years after my second marriage ended for the last time. I say last time as it confirms my point. I was having a conversation with a friend or more accurately I was verbalizing the chats that had been entertaining each other in my head and had become so loud I needed to let them all out. I was reminiscing about all the wonderful parts, episodes of the fallen relationship that highlighted when I thought times were perfect.

I realized that through most of those times, I was by myself in a sense that he was not physically around. It was quite the moment to finally understand that it hadn't been him necessarily I was grieving but what my life with him represented. The times of connecting with my soul through Nature, activities, places we lived. I was sad because of what I thought was the loss of a part of me, not him.

◆◆◆

Getting myself out of the way....

Here in the warmth of an early January afternoon protected from the winds of inevitable change blowing though the Grandmother Cedars outside my living room window. standing tall, watching, protecting. There is a knowing, that there is no growing backwards. Only onwards and up. Like me, time spent here in this home of two years. From a place of uncertainty subtly caressing my subconscious need to control.

The illusion that only through this control can the outcome be deemed worthy of stature. I am slowly brought back from a well-deserved afternoon nap on the couch by what seems to be the more insistent humming of the inner workings of the refrigerator, the whirling emanating from 3 foot electric heater and the realization that although life has made itself clear that my time in this home is coming to an end ,it is also time to prepare to transfer all I have come to learn within to the next leg of the journey.

You see it doesn't matter at the end of the day the how's and whys of it all, what matters is the belief and determination in which I act upon the outcomes. This determines whether it has all truly carried the purpose for which it was intended. Acknowledging this belief from a place of purity that resides in the heart, not the mind. I moved to this secluded home only two years before. Giving thanks to the Universe, Creator, my Ancestors, my guides for such a sacred and what most are finding out today scarce commodity of physical locality in which to do the unbeknownst to me at the time, the intended internal work.

Whatever that work looks like now seems to have a different introduction to it. I have spent what has felt like forever at different times in earnest plea to not fail, to not have it, me been all for nothing. The black feathered friends have arrived for their afternoon snack. Like I mentioned before, it started with a couple crows showing up checking me out. Becoming brave enough to allow me to sit with them and share moments with snacks. I think it was a mate and its partner first.

I would watch holding my breath as the smaller one would stand near the larger one with head down in quiet. Waiting for the larger one to acknowledge and then with its beak gently groom between the feathers lain on its head.

With the skilled touch of a loved one who has done this so many times before, it would pick out the yuckiness from the corners of the wee one's eyes. The absolute unconditional trust the smaller one whom I named Steve had shown was quite inspiring. Steve eventually broadened his trust to me and If I sat perfectly still, while looking the other way with my hand outstretched bearing a treat, he would do his little three step scurry/ dance back and forth until he was sure he had the right angle on it then snatch the goods from between my fingers. I would then in delight say" good job Steve. I knew you could do it".

The next spring, He never came back because of why. I don't know can only hazard a guess. Nature doing what is needed to be done? Or maybe he has but is bigger now and I don't recognize him. I think once in awhile I see him based on some of the familiar behaviors exhibited. Like greeting me when I pull up to park with the car then after a wave of my hand saying, "come on let's go get a snack," he flies with me over my head. very close I might add which on occasion has caused him to contact my hair. As a matter of fact, the other day while I was out front talking with my neighbour when a "Steve" landed on the sidewalk between the two of us and proceeded to waddle onto the street behind my car. I was like" Steve! Get off the road before you get hit" and low and behold he abruptly turned around, sauntered back onto the sidewalk then into my front yard.

I laughed so hard!! The neighbour just shook his head chuckling. So perfect. I couldn't have planned that. "If you had not been here to see that, I don't think you would have believed me" I told him.

More have recently started to show up. If they think its their turn they cry. "No shouting "I'd say and only when they were quiet would the days treats whether be bits of bread, leftover supper, or the like was laid out.

Walmart has these rings of kubasa on special and if I cut them thin enough, I could get three to four days of servings for them. It has become part of my daily routine. Do the morning rituals that involve the cleansing, clearing of bodily functions.

Brush the sweaters of my teeth that found their way during the night. Down the mason jar concoction of filtered water, greens powder and a healthy squeeze of fresh lemon. Then of course between all these movements check Facebook or the ole FB as I like to call it.

Never know I might have missed something. Hahaha. On more than one occasion it has been the only source of information via friends and family posts about recent events such as a Passing of a relative or a celebration of another loved one. Both require equal reverence and acknowledgement in my opinion. Text good morning to my boys.

A ritual that when for whatever reason I don't do first thing will create thoughts in my head that affirm I am not being a good mother if I don't do this. That they won't know how much I am constantly thinking of them not just when I wake but throughout my days until the last thoughts floating across my frontal lobe before I allow myself the well-deserved rest time to come.

Make the bed. A task I related to as a younger version of myself that was a unnecessary chore. That perception changed during the first fast I participated in back in 2000. One of the Women leaders who looked after us mentioned it was important to make our sleeping spot up as soon as we rose to prevent any of the possible nighttime not so good spirits to enter between the blankets.

So, whether I really believed it or not at the time I don't remember but what I did get from that act over time was a feeling of discipline.

Practicing it at home became a regular routine. Frankly I came to like it as it would give me a sense of accomplishment to start the day and to take that further it also paired well with my need on occasion to practice what some would call OCD behaviors. These usually presented themselves when I was under stress, emotional, feeling very stirred up in my insides.

During my first marriage it was so bad that my clothes were all hung colour co-ordinated, whenever we had guests and someone used the washroom, I would follow in right after and wipe down sink, doorknob, straighten the hand towel than do a last look before I could breathe comfortably. My husband used to tease me in front of people by throwing a magazine in the middle of the living room floor saying, "want to see Heidi go crazy?"

I swear I would have to sit on my hands for as long as I could before it would become too much before I snatched it up putting it back in its proper place in that lower shelf of the coffee table. The top of the table was glass so needless to say the arrangement of magazines needed to be just right. A therapist told me a while later that the main reason behaviors like mine occurred was because it was a coping mechanism to try to create a false sense of control on the outside to subdue the feelings of loss of this control that screamed inside me.

I will say that today because of working the issues that stood in the way in my mind from Trauma experiences, I can now leave the dishes in the sink longer than an hour and even overnight if need be!! Next, opening the blinds.

There's usually one perched atop the back of the chair or on the stairs outside my kitchen window. Peering intently through the glass with its head cocked to one side revealing its glistening black marble-like eye as if to say, "are you in there?' it then begins moving about trying to get a better look, to get my attention. When I finally spot Him, I dig out the container from the fridge that is now the official Crow food storage one and proceed to meal out the rations.

I open the door asking" is it snack time "and he'll hop down from his perch eyeing me up to see where I lay out breakfast. A couple of them have become accustomed to entering the doorway just enough to take the snack off the plate I put on the floor after I them 'Come get your snack". This fella Steve though eats out of my hand. I have to say it has been the purest of pleasures over the last couple years experiencing the unique evolution of interactions that make my days.

In the times when I have felt like I was at my most alone, in fear, in uncertainty and yes even in anger, these moments with these intelligent beings have brought me around. Every time. After our ritual it feels like once again for a moment all is right in my world and exactly as its supposed to be. It didn't take me long to know that even though my brain would try to tell me that I was there helping them during the rainy, cold, hot times with sustenance. Ha, another prime example of ego. They've known all along it's been the other way around. They truly have there for me. They were sent by the Ones I had pleaded to for help.

As the days have gone by and the times of peace and stillness have come into my days staying a bit longer with each visit, they appear less and less. And so, now as I continue to prepare for my transition to wherever I will be living at some point during this year following my last chemo treatment at the end of this month, only the one most wise still lands on the step outside peering in, waiting for the snack. I hope I am ready. I will trust in the growth my Spirit has taken on, stretching upwards to the outside world once again, detaching from my story as it is becoming more and more not about me anymore. Stepping aside so the ways of it can be received freely by those whose own search in Self is waiting. Waiting to catch a glimpse through their window for the encouragement, the hope, and the faith in their purposefulness

◆◆◆

Being in the state of....

The time of seasonal stillness has come. It used to have a general timeline one could rely on and prepare for but as of late with the intensifying unsettling of humanity and all its parts, it now decides when enough is enough. Like a stern yet loving parent that needs to put their unruly child into a time-out to think about their behavior.

This season we traditionally call winter finally dons the cap by bringing in once again the deep chill which causes all living beings to instinctively crawl into their dens of comfort and security. I get it. Will go out on a limb and say I understand.

The animals are scarce now. The yard needs no work, no preparation yet. There is no job to pick out clothes, a lunch to pack, no obligations to show up on time for.

The children are grown and my role in supporting their day-to-day experiences has calmed to a lull. There is no direction given yet as to where I'm moving next. So, I will wait. I will rest, my mind, my body, keeping my thoughts clear. heart still, to hear with clarity the next list of instructions. I can do this all without having to move away from the rhythm. I will accept the opportunity to embrace with optimism and gratitude the result of all the healing thus far.

I will take direction from the air that settles into a sense of quiet. I have done the work. It is time to allow myself to feel the benefits of it fully. No need to look ahead, no need to really look back except in an unattached reflection. I give myself permission to not move my mind in any direction outside the self that is Source found. "Do nothing "I tell myself.

"Quit looking for distractions. Have another nap, another cup of tea perhaps.' I can't remember ever being here in this. The fact that I am is statement to the worthiness of my trek. I need to remember that more often. And so, I shall start now. They say its never too late.

I concur. If I had thought that 100 percent, the spark that has flared throughout to reignite the desire to live not just survive would have been snuffed along time ago. I was always under the impression that if I was not "doing" then I was not being. On the contrary, From the first breath leaving the womb I have been in a constant state of being.

My life has been the process of unlearning, disconnecting from others' perceptions of how this Beings journey should be played out. I allow myself to let that all go. Let it go into the ether. In a most unfamiliar yet ironically familiar way that has the potential to bring personal awareness into a world of my perceptive reality, I continue to invite through the reaching out in prayer and the consciousness for the courage, strength and understanding that enables me to walk through the days however they may look or feel.

Kindness really is everything....

I readily admit that I have not been, kind that is, many times in my life. To myself, with those I thought I was protecting myself from. The reasons I tell myself have varied. The excuses I carried, wrapped up in different ways. Through times of survival, memories of past. I justified. I condemned. Not only others, but also and some would say Moreso myself. I share this not to say this Visitor has come and hopefully now gone is the result of this state.

Only that I have had the opportunity during this time to finally understand. I have been shown in the most genuine way the reflections of all the interactions with the world around me these past 6 months. I had finally come out of a year and a half of injury and rehabilitation, from an isolation of the mind mostly, when I started my last employment. I thought absolutely without a shadow of a doubt that this was it. YAY!!

The creator had heard and answered my deepest prayers. All my hopes and dreams for that everlasting job that was not only my passion but the one that would take me long into my twilight time with ease. I finally had what It felt in my heart the perfect home. Peaceful, balanced.

My relationships with two of my sons had somewhat evolved into the place of wellness, forgiveness, and re-connection that my Soul had craved for, needed with every fibre of my being for over 30 years. All the mental, emotional, physical, and spiritual work I had done in its many forms had come full circle. Well guess what.

The work never stops. I was so happy for this new lease on life. I was also so scared. I slowly started to regress back into who I had not wanted to be at the lowest times in my life. What is that they say about inner peace? The meditation Master can be unphased up on the mountain all by themselves, but can they carry that same peace whilst walking amongst the chaos down below? I was in such fear that all "this" would disappear that I fell back into trying to become indispensable.

I threw my all and more into everything I did at work. Was attempting to do not only my job but was pushing my way to lessen the loads of others around. I was constantly looking for assurance and approval from my manager, the store manager, even the team that I would last out my days there. And I got it. It was acknowledged through emails from the higher ups, in customer comment cards, and by other staff. But where I failed was to have an awareness of the ripple affect this created.

I was so focused on what I needed to do that I did not see around me in clarity. I did not see where some of the best ways I could have been kind was to allow others to fall on their face so to speak, allow others the opportunity to learn what they were there to learn.

Back in the Sundance days I tried being for all. It was in my 3rd year during the 4 prep days before we were going to dance in. One of the women leaders had brought me aside and said "its good you are so dedicated and want to help so much. But if you do it all, how will those that need experience what they are meant to while they are here?" 7 days into my new employment came the news. Within two hours after the CT scan with contrast my family Doctor called. The diagnosis was not good. He just kept repeating" I'm so sorry Heidi." It was discovered I had me a body visitor just above my right ovary. Yep, the C word.

To this day I don't even like to give it the attention of a first letter capitalization. I do not want to give it any more attention or recognition it is asking for. The Doctor said it was of the intestinal nature stemming from most commonly the ovarian type. I was going to need a biopsy to confirm followed by more tests, chemo, surgery, more chemo and then who knew.

I am grateful today that even though the job ended. Even after my employers said they would support me, that they terminated me without cause 3 weeks before the intensive cancer surgery was to happen. That they acted in such a way as to stomp on my Human rights and freedoms (according to the Tribunal), In this moment now I can humbly admit the Good Creator was clearing the path once again since I couldn't seem to get out of my own way and once again, I was unkind. I became judgemental of them. Criticizing m of the many customers in my head.

I was telling myself that they were acting so entitled and couldn't they see on the grand scheme of things how all our priorities were askew. I was becoming frustrated with what I saw all around me behaviors that seemed to only come from a place of selfishness, greed and lack of the willingness to understand and have compassion for people other than themselves.

As I put this thought down it occurs to me that whatever I was judging about "them" was exactly what I was being myself. Ha! Oh my... That character defect raised itself up in the way that it allowed me to put on the blame and anger mask. Why do we do that, why does it feel so instinctual to go there first? Does it make it easier to go back into comfort.

To avoid the truth of what the discomfort will reveal. I think so. I know while I was employed and kept myself so busy in my head and exhausted in the body, I didn't have to admit I was scared. I could almost pretend I was looking in from the outside. Even though what my previous employer had done was so wrong on the humanity level aspect, on the Universal plane maybe it was what was needed for me come back into the reason I was here?

Not to say that I change my mind about standing up for myself. I just need to do it in a good way. This journey has taken me to the very depth of my being in a way that nothing else ever could. I have grieved in ways I never thought I would. Looked into the illusions I have carried in both the past and still now. I have become willing once gain to stop attempting to control the outcome of which I have no say.

Most importantly, by slowly seeing where my human frailties lie, I can take notice of others without taking it on personally their behavioral suffering. This last one has been as of late been easier than I thought it would be. As a result of my world being turned around, I am now having to look elsewhere for living accommodation. I chose to reach out to the many Facebook housing sites with an ad. No sooner had I posted when there was a response that was so judgemental, hurtful, and blaming, accusing me of not being authentic in the reasons for my quest and demanding Dr proof etc. that I was astounded.

My very first knee jerk reaction was to defend myself. Which I did in honesty. Her follow-up reactions describing how her mom has cancer. she found her father passed away and her brother was in another country while still cutting, judging me for what she felt was my ineptitude to be able to provide for myself and be financially secure over the years so I wouldn't end up in this state was to a final moment of my heart moving from defensiveness to that of compassion. I immediately responded apologizing for my defense without so much as considering the pain she must be in regarding her circumstances.

I then took ownership of how unfair that was of me as a member of a community that professes to be a forum of support in which that I had not done so. What a shift within me this created. It felt like the last of any attachment to that aspect of wounded self fell away. what a gift.

A few days later, I was discussing some of my journey these last 6 months with a neighbour sharing only the gratitude I feel for all that has supported my time here. My genuine desire and determination to stay in gratitude and positivity while still being able to be truthful and acknowledge all other feelings that surge through me.

He was quite taken aback that I was able to do so with such willingness without attachment to the outwardly appearance of suffering. I simply replied" The universe hasn't brought me this far to drop me on my head otherwise it would have provided a helmet. Do you see a helmet! I have always had food in my mouth, a roof over my head, support when needed unless I made the choice to not accept it." I used to say this a time ago to bring myself out of the heaviness and fear I would feel but today I can share this as the truth my Soul has found.

During this time of travel, I have now found the kindness with which I speak. Yes, for others but most importantly for myself. Albeit not practised as much or as often as my being most certainly deserves but practised none the less. For without this I cannot truly carry out the purpose of my existence. Without the practice of this compassion within, I cannot honor my commitment I made with the good Creator long before I entered this realm.

The simple truth of how we as human beings, Soul relatives, will find our way out of the darkness and into the light. The light that I have seen radiate throughout my life even when I didn't recognize it. The light I felt while being wrapped in other cultures teachings from around the world. Whatever land I have set my footsteps on, the light has ALL-ways had the same name. They call it LOVE.

I have personally felt this love in many unexpected ways. the most usual has been at various moments in my life when I am deeply processing whether be a dilemma or unresolved feeling, I will be walking about anywhere and I mean ANYWHERE, when a heart will show itself. In a paint blob, in the natural bark on a tree. Many heart stones over the years I have collected.

Only to re-distribute them. While I was working at the Spa in Victoria, I had so many that for thanksgiving I gave one to every Massage and body worker in the Spa.

One time while I was at work in the produce department cutting and preparing ready to grab fruit trays, I sliced open a watermelon and there it was, another reminder for me that I was loved and to trust this gift from the Universe. Which I've come to learn speaks to me in though some might think in an odd way but speaks in a manner I can relate to. Fear being the opposite of faith....
What a difference a day. a moment. an event in time can make.

A prime example of the realities showing evidence of what a fickle bunch we two-legged are. It's been a few days since I have put words to paper. I am waiting. Waiting for the message to reveal itself on how next to proceed. A lot has happened during this time away from the laptop. One of my sons whom I love with all my heart has become another statistic in the whole "Employer manipulating the system and relying on the naiveness of him to achieve their own unethical goal "situation.

 And of course, I don my mom hat on, check to make sure it is snug, tilted just right to one side yet firmly in place. This is the one I reserve for in times of feeling the need to rescue, create a scenario in which I feel I am by combining it with my accessory justice cape along with it am equipped to processed righting wrongs.

 I immediately swing into action pulling out all the stops in my research techniques, foraging my brain for long lost bits of Canadian law I had studied while in school so I could be supporting him in standing up for his rights and the ways in which to achieve that. I jump in with all the zeal I readily have on hand for anything I fully believe in.

 I was fired up to say the least. Even though ultimately the outcome of his experience is divinely guided, and he is the one that must do the work, I needed to feel like I could help him take control over a situation that would not only benefit him in the long run but also allow for personal growth and success in the future.

I spent a few nights sleepless going over and over in my mind all the ways his employer was crossing the line then redefining them for selfish gains. Racking my already overloaded thoughts for anything, any tidbit of information I may have overlooked.

It took me a good week to finally decide I had done all I could do, and the rest was up to all those directly involved and yet to show up in the experience. That was exhausting! I was back to sleeping again. Back to feeling like could breathe, like whoever was standing on my chest while yelling in my head AKA my friend anxiety, was gone.

I could now focus once again on my own healing. During this, from what seemed like a very subtle exposure, fear in its guise of just overtiredness, had started to creep in again but now it was about the events starting to unfold in my life that would affect me directly. Where was I going to live when I was better. My landlady had started recently making noises about how her daughter was going to be moving in once she finished University, that her brother would be visiting from Hong Kong more often upstairs.

He didn't like that he had to be mindful of a tenant downstairs and so did not want me here anymore. I had known for the last year that this would not be my forever home and that it would not be easy to find affordable housing in a short time, so I had started to put feelers out, got my name on the appropriate waiting lists for someone needing lower income housing. Unfortunately, I had never saved for retirement.

Sure, at times in the last 10 years I had little nest eggs that would in the event I lost my source of income I would be ok for three months but overall, between the raising children by myself while not earning any worthwhile income to later years when I finally was able to, so much changed. The vibration of financial greed in the world was showing its true self much more blatantly than any time I had seen before. I was astounded at my luck when because of venturing out into new kinds of employment that I had found what seemed like my golden goose.

I was sure it was now going to last, that I had finally come into my own. It wasn't too late for me. I had started out my independent financial journey at 17. Carrying my firstborn and 5 dollars in my pocket into an office seeking government assistance. Followed by years of on and off the Dole, bringing more children into the world, eating once every couple day so there was enough for the boys every meal.

All the while finding ways to keep a roof over our heads both in marriage and out. I used to say that even when I was married, I was still a single parent. Once sobriety seemed to stick. my life started to change for the better. Each phase, 4-year cycle it seemed was becoming more solid. through education, perseverance, commitment, and many hours of hanging on by the thread to blind faith, I had arrived.

Not sure what the name of the destination was but I didn't care. As a single woman with only financial responsibilities of Self now, I took the trips, splurged on good food, adventures, housing, all the while telling myself I would start saving later. It just did not ever occur to me in any way that time would creep up on me carrying with it unique circumstances evolving out of natural aging and the world, would abruptly cut short this success.

But later never came. I was injured at work, my body breaking down and then as I mentioned before, cancer came to visit. So here I sit, one more treatment to go, no prospect of employment of any kind once better. My last employer took care of that. I have absolutely no idea how I am going to be able to afford the rent where I am at presently very soon.

No savings and despite the overwhelming support of others spurred on by my youngest sister setting up a Go fund me page. It isn't enough. When it will come time to switch my source of income back once again to relying on the government sure I will be able to pay the rent, I just won/t be eating or having a phone, transportation, or any other basic needs. Once I must leave this sanctuary of the last two years where will I go?

I know, I know, be positive, have faith, review the words I shared with my neighbour. Here's the thing; I am scared. I do need to feel that too while heading towards that faith door. Everywhere the rents were getting higher and higher.

Any low-income housing there was at least a 5-year waiting list. I would not last that long. The fear of becoming homeless like so many others in the encampments all around the cities and suburbs seems to be looming up to stare me in the face. So how do I distract myself? My son tells me of another staff member that was terminated at his old work unfairly even while his situation had not come to resolution yet and once again, I jump into action to research and provide all the information I could on how she could fight it.

Thinking this is my calling. I am meant to be an advocate for those that need help navigating the system for support. Not realizing I had not truly been that for myself as of late. At the end of the day when I am so exhausted physically from having gone through my second last chemo treatment only a week ago, my mind will not quiet after I lay down. In fact, it seems to start raising its voice just one octave at time over an hour and a half of tossing and turning until I can't take it anymore. "Ok Creator "I say out loud "I really need your help to let this go. I can't do any more sleepless nights".

As I continue to talk aloud to Creator, to myself, another ah ha moment. I realize I am mad, not just angry. And not just on behalf of them but because what their experiences are triggering in me. I was not able to stand up for myself with my former employer.

Sure, I have filed a Human Rights complaint but that will take months to be even looked at. In the meantime, I feel powerless. I had not been able to make them accountable for their actions. A least not in the time frame I want it to happen in. They took away my job security and by doing so have left me in the position of the very real possibility of residing in the summertime shelter I store away in the trunk of the car for those care-free days of intertwining with Nature. I feel like there is no one to fight for me.

That I have no means of being able to control the narrative in my life which now more than ever seems so important to my mental, emotional well-being. I also realize that I had been so focused on trying not to have any stress during my recovery that I haven't allowed myself the very real part of working through loss.

The loss of what my job had represented for me. The potential of finally getting it right before it's too late, of not just being able to survive but to live without fear. I had glazed over the very healthy part of grieving that was one of the 5 stages. Anger…. I am pissed right fucking off!

 There, I've said it....I'm pissed at the ex-employer; I am pissed that I have no recourse other than Human Rights. I had very early on talked to a lawyer and I was told they were my only option. And I am pissed at myself… That somehow, I allowed this all to happen or manifested it in some way.

 I had been so busy attempting to stay in the present, in positivity (which some have labeled false positivity) so as not to hinder recovery that I avoided the very real aspects of this deep-seated rage that has been festering this whole time.

Everyone around me has been in their own caring way voicing how strong I am being, how amazed they are that I am taking and dealing with this experience in such an upbeat way. That this attitude of constant application of only the best most positive thoughts, words, and actions, will guarantee the success of a full recovery.

I feel like I have failed though, in my efforts to remain as comfortable as possible without consequence I missed this imperative step. The acknowledgement of anger, of fear, of sadness. This cuts to the core. I swore after what I presumed to be needless suffering occurring at the hands of the succession of relationships, previous employment prior to this last one and yes even by those who professed to love me within my own family, that I would not fall prey again.

That I would stand up, be heard, and be accounted for. I would raise my fist in the air in solidarity with the woman warriors of my time singing the honor song that was a message of strength. A song that came to a Mt Currie Elder in a dream to support her peoples so many years ago. A long standing traditional Lil'wat Territory song that came from a place of support, not aggression or blame.

I also know I can choose to stay mad long after it is a necessary step and have it become a liability, or I can use it constructively. I choose the latter and I am grateful to be able to recognize what has just transpired.

Funny how it all starts with the tiniest degree of willingness. It's that seemingly unimportant decision that can create such a profound change in perspective in what feels like a very short time that brings a stillness back into my Being. Will my son ever truly know how much his experience has allowed me to move forward in this moment.

I believe I will tell him one day, maybe best before he reads it, I don't know. I best just get out of the way and let Creator decide how that will play out since he already has the master plan in the works anyways.

I do know however I no longer feel powerless. I feel it's because I was able to have the courage to ask Creator for help, that the physical feeling of wanting to scream at the top of my lungs has passed for now. I guess it's appropriate I am finally here in this realization. I hope it means I once again have looked within and taken stock of the Humanness that is still evolving as long as I draw a breath. I have not graduated, nor will I in this lifetime so I best get on with it.

This phrase however does not mean suck it up. It means trudge forward. When I had first heard the phrase ". as we trudge the road…" It would conjure up a vision of one dressed in the heaviest of clothing apparel, lifting with great effort every foot to plow through waist high snow to get to the next spot. I have since learned that the word Trudge means is "to walk with purpose"

So, get on with it I shall, with the business of continued willingness to take the next right step. Knowing that this will eventually once again lead me back onto the path of my authentic self, living my best life at any given moment regardless of external circumstance. For there is nothing more then that is there.

Gift from a Hummingbird Relative....

Its only 8;30 in the morning and already the day have been full. The Spirits or Creator not sure which, woke me out of a sound sleep earlier. Maybe they are one in the same? I guess it depends on the cultural belief one carries. As does all moment-to-moment translations of symbolic events in an individual's life. How does the translation feel in the inner knowing aspects of the Self.

As soon as my eyes were open fully rested, I told myself." Don't waste the day, Heidi. "And I was up. Little did I know the powerful moments that were about to unfold before me. One look outside into the dark sky being slowly illuminated on the horizon told me time to bundle up, get out there, light a smudge and watch the sunrise. I did as the voice within instructed.

Wrapped in layers of scarves, hat, cozy knee length fuzzy hoodie and with extra comfort my legs entwined with one of those soft lap blankets made from the kind of material that if in the dryer too long it would start to smell like it was melting, I perched myself on the stairs leading up to the upper deck, to get the best view.

Smudge lit and, on my lap, my phone by my side in the event of the opportunity to take that WOW, would you just look at that amazing sunrise photo.

As the sky grew lighter and the clouds that wisped into the blue radiated the reddish orange hue of the sun I sat in prayer. Giving thanks to each item and circumstance that came into my heart to be spoken. I have so much to be grateful for the list can seemingly be endless but here were some very pertinent ones that I needed to recognize right now.

Some of which is the courage within myself and those in which I was speaking of to change from where we were to where we are now in our growth. I was so focused on these prayers and thoughts that at one point I started thinking about how maybe it was time to fast again. Who would take care of me the where and when's of it all. I forgot the smudge was lit. That this smoke from the medicine was making its way up to the Creator in a visual prayerful way.

As soon as I realized this, I also put forth the giving up the control of how it would look to the powers that be and if even it was meant to happen in the first place. I created the space in my words that if so to please show me the signs. It was then I saw how light it was now becoming and simultaneously heard the morning call of the local hummingbirds in the cedars nearby.

Yes! I told myself, time to put their feeder out. It had been so cold out these last few days that I have been bringing the feeder in at night to stay liquified and then they would have fresh breakfast in the morning. I quickly gathered all my "stuff" up and headed back into the house.

Grabbed the feeder off the counter by the door and headed back out to hang it. As I was putting it up in its usual spot, I noticed out of the corner of my eye on the cement at the bottom of my steps to ground level. what looked like a crumpled old leaf? I didn't have my glasses on so I couldn't make it out clearly but as I approached it my heart sank. It was one of the hummingbirds. I picked it up and held it, her in the palm of my hand.

She was so still and even though her body was not ice cold I knew she was gone. She couldn't have weighed more then an ounce. Even with the layers of iridescent green feathers that covered her. My heart broke. The waves of grief suddenly appeared. Overflowing into tears and cries of apologies. Had I done something wrong to cause this to happen. Should I not have been providing winter sustenance and maybe she would have traveled to a warmer climate?

Did I not get the food out in time that she no longer had the nutrients needed to keep her body warm? Then I heard a voice inside me. it was Uncles' voice. Reminding me of how when an animal gives themselves to you in death, they are answering your prayers to take away any suffering you had wanted to let go of. My words of grief through tears running down my face went from that of sorrow to giving thanks for her sacrifice.

For her journey. All the while crying from a deep place in my core, I lay her on a bed of sage and tobacco in a red cloth preparing her for her final resting place of physicality. I wished for her to now forever be warm, have all the nourishment she wanted while being forever in the sun.

I approached Grandmother Cedar in the back yard where this Annas hummingbird sat many a day amid her fronds and silently offered her up to be welcomed back amongst her roots. The ceremony was complete.

The grief had subsided within me, and I now felt a sense of reverence for what I had just been a part of. Such a gift this day. I knew instinctively when I found her that there was a message, but I needed to weave myself through the whole process. The meaning behind her giving of herself in this most sacred way but I still felt I needed to research it a bit more.

As I read through the various spiritual meanings about hummingbirds about death, there appeared tidbits that I immediately connected to. I guess my search was more to affirm what I hadn't yet put into words and I for sure didn't want to be making anything up for my convenience.

There was so much in her message, but I will simplify it to this:

"There is change coming, not just with only having one chemo treatment left but in what it seems to be pretty much all areas of my life. With this change there is a necessity to fully embrace it, the need to let go of what no longer serves. The letting go of ideas, behaviors, attitudes, and belief systems. Those that served their purpose to support me into coming into this moment right here, right now have lived their life. Time to release them with gratitude, without remorse or guilt, just as this beautiful feathered relative shared with me in the day to day her journey from joy, hopefulness, innocence, and love to her crossing into the realm of spirit letting me go. Spirits were telling me that the transitioning was coming to ready myself only in acceptance and understanding and the rest will follow. There is no need to try to analyze all the details in hopes of this understanding. The only requirement is surrender. In this act the freedom continues to flow and with this gift of freedom comes peace. That feeling within the heart chakra region that feels like one has just experienced a huge sigh of relief invoking calm...."

Time to feed the Crows. they seem very quiet today, as if they know there has been a transition. That the circle of life for one of their feathered relatives had just been the reason for a powerful sacred death ceremony just moments before their arrival. As I spread out their organic white cheddar mac n cheese so they all could have access to it, they watched me with those ever-knowing marble like black eyes in respect.

When I stepped back a few paces, their usual frenzied scramble to the food is noticeably absent. Instead, it is replaced with a hesitant sideways approach as if to attempt as little disruption to the space as possible. There is no usual flapping of the wings at each other to show who's in charge. The ground is cleared in moments, so quickly in fact I wondered for a second if I had put anything out yet. As I go about my day, it feels like I have new eyes.

I am noticing, more aware it seems of everything around me. The vibrancy of the vegetables at the local market. Even though they were reduced to clear because of very minor imperfections, they have always been the ones I gravitate towards first. Not just for price but sometimes I would find different items that normally I wouldn't see anywhere else.

At the library I am engaged in more conversation then normal with the two staff behind the counter. The natural flow of connection comes easier than most days. I approach my street slowly driving up the street incline. I am moved by the contrast of the stark white horizontal wispy clouds against the backdrop of the crisp blue sky.

A leisurely afternoon that involves the dicing and slicing. The preparation for an abundance of stir fry. Seems to have a much more decadent flavour than I normally managed to put together. As I clear the last of it off my plate for the third time, I said out loud to Creator" that was so good!! Thank you!!"

The day finally ends with the setting of the sun illuminating the skies holding Grandmother Moon with the most astonishing lavender hue that I have ever seen. I am in awe of the day, this moment, this warmth flowing through me. Once again, I share out loud to the Universe the sincerest gratitude that has been wrapped in grace surrounding my heart. I feel spent.

Spent but content and looking forward to a night of warmth wrapped in the Afghans my sisters have made themselves as an expression of their Love for me. A night of feeling once again the safety within my home being looked in on periodically by Ones from the other side.

That's good stuff....

I will say I am not going to miss the regular insertion of the IV needle either in my hand or just above my inner wrist area which was then taped down to keep the needle stable so the flow of chemicals that has been set to drip accordingly was not impeded. After flushing the needle with a saline solution, the first infusion is Benadryl which they use to expand the body's cells so the chemo can enter more readily.

With each treatment I found the IV insertion site within 20 minutes would start to feel like a cold burn. So, they would then wrap the area with a hot cloth. Once this feeling calmed down the Benadryl would kick in and I'd have me nap for a bit. This nap was only because after experiencing one of the side effects of the Benadryl was, I would get severe restless leg on the right side of my body. After the second of 6 cycles I figured out a cure for that though.

A friend makes this non-THC containing CBD spray and I would massage it onto both legs before I went to the clinic. Now that was the cats meow. Worked like a hot dang to eliminate the issue! I would instinctively come around just before it was time to start the chemo drip. Sometimes I would fade off again for a bit but most times.

By this stage my lower back would start to burn from nerve pain. A succession would follow of bathroom visits, chatting it up with someone around me while counting down the time.

After the chemo they would then flush and start a steroid drip for about 20 minutes before finishing with another flush. This whole process lasted approximately 5 and a half hours. The first 3 days after each treatment I would generally feel okay overall considering.

Part of that was because of the oral steroid I was needing to take in the morning and night for those days. When it came to the very brief moments of nausea however, I chose not to use their prescription, instead I would consume a lozenge that I had made myself which consisted of Slippery Elm powder and Manuka Honey.

As soon as I would start to feel the nausea, I would slowly dissolve it in my mouth and the side effect would go away until the next day. This lozenge also helped with the sore throat and any sores in the mouth that would arise. I would apply straight Mauka honey on a lip blister that would pop up and it would heal within a day. As for the heavy white coating on the tongue caused by what they call Chemo Thrush, I took regularly a high-grade professional line of a probiotic.

The only side effect I had to utilize western medicine for was the excruciating intense burning nerve pain that would commence around the fourth day for a couple days. It would start in the mid drift, radiate into the pelvis area before making its way down my inner and back of my thighs into my feet. Tylenol, naproxen, even my usual go to of drops of Frankincense essential oil under the tongue for pain didn't even put a dent in it.

I gratefully accepted the Hydro-morphine tablets to take for that! As a recovering addict / alcoholic it was important to me to only take it at night before bed. This enabled my body to get some much-needed rest for which I am eternally grateful for a couple nights. On or around the 7th day is when I would start to feel like I'm coming back.

Those moments of thought during chemo week where I am unsure whether I can make it through, dissipates to be replaced with Phew now follows a 2 week reprieve. I believe there is a time and a place for everything in the medicine world. That most therapies can co-exist if done so in a good way. I tell people if I break my leg I am going to get a cast, consume some of the good pain killers until such time as it eases up enough, I switch to the Homeopathic Arnica internally addressing the trauma of the injury alongside a topical of a natural cream or oil that contains Comfrey in it to help heal the break.

The Elders call Comfrey the Bone/ wound knitter. There have been stories from different ones that told of back during the fighting in the attempt to regain the land and ways back, when a warrior would come back to camp with a big wound or break, the medicine person would stuff or wrap it with a comfrey leaf then send them back out.

◆◆◆

Gratitude is in the action....

The ceremonial bells honouring the end of my last treatment have been rung. The clinic has this ritual when they unhook you for that last time from your IV, they give you these bells that are like those of the old days where the town Crier went through the streets announcing the news. You get to ring them for as long as you want.
 The Last treatment completed yesterday. So many mixed thoughts words, and actions this last week leading up to it.

 Feels like it has been probably one of the most challenging emotionally for me, believe it or not. One would think all the phases of these last 6 months brought their own and yes, they did but as always it seems with my ways of coping in the any life events I have had, it has repeatedly been when I am only a few hairs away from the finish line that becomes the hardest place to be. To continue all the steps that enable peace, calm, acceptance, and clarity to reign.

 I feel it's because as I get closer to the completion of said experience the concept of hanging on however I can for just this minute because the end seems so far away is no longer the reality. The reality becomes one of the unknown once again. Will all this have worked in the way I want it to? The way Creator intended for a long and happy recovered life??

Will the other shoe drop down the road and if so, when? Will I be able to reside completely in that place of wholeness mentally emotionally physically and spiritually? All the unknowns show themselves more clearly. So, during the last week I was very tearful at the drop of a hat, short tempered while driving as well as my physical limitations, judgemental of myself and others.

Today I am shaky (one of the side-affects) but still ever so grateful. During this journey many people have commented on how such an inspiration I am and so grateful for my sharing of this time with them, but I say to them over and over this has been quite the team effort.

Those moments and sometimes hours of feeling so scared, alone, and unsure have only been overcome by hearing, seeing the encouragement, support, and unconditional love from everyone sent from the good Creator to join me on this walk. The greatest gift has been my boys Shawne and Andrew who not only have been with me every step of the way in the best way they could but were also able to be with me via facetime at the end of the last chemo treatment.

They will never know I think just how much I needed, that my heart needed to have them with me in whatever way they could to finish this part. Not just for the end of treatments for me but hopefully the end to their fears and sadness that they have been through up until this moment.

They have been so very strong! I have felt their strength and their logical fears whilst looking into their eyes. I have seen their deep love for me. I had spent all 6 treatments unaccompanied so to have my sons with me to close them out was the absolute perfect moment I could have possibly wished for and for the first time I shed tears of joy of relief, of grief, gratitude, and prayers in public.

All the thoughts of the unknowns I have once again put on the back burner and am in the moment, I am choosing to live the feelings of completion. To reflect on the past six months without attachment. And to relish in the vibrations of love and kindness that grew roots on this path. The processing of the teachings, the messaging and the constants will take their time revealing themselves. Just as some 5-20 years later the words of my Elders, Uncles and the like still come to light in an ah ha moment now and again.

There will be a time maybe once more when this experience will no longer be about me. It will become the message for others that make themselves available to receive by asking. I just need to remember that when it feels like I'm hitting the wall every now and again. Our experiences are not meant to be pushed upon others when we think we see the need to because we have the answers.

As much as we have compassion and hope for them if we repeatedly heap our knowledge upon them without their asking, we deny them the opportunity to honour their commitment with the Good Creator. Once again Uncles words come to my mind "It is not our job to tell someone how to take their place in the medicine wheel". In laymen's terms, its none of our business unless asked for our opinion.

Even then it is only our opinion we share. If we keep on repeating ourselves regardless of our desire for them to reach optimal wellness, wholeness, we are no longer just sharing, we are trying to control, get them to see our way. We are trying to fix them and as a result disempowering them. This realization I have had to remind myself of not only through the years of motherhood when I saw my children hurting, but even these last 6 months.

When I had found ways to cope with the side affects of chemo with natural supplements, ways to take care of my Spiritual, mental, and emotional aspects, it would take everything I had to not share them uninvited with other cancer patients when I would hear them chatting in the chemo pod next to me.

As a matter of fact, during my last treatment yesterday the spouse of the one receiving his first treatment kept wandering over and would talk to me and I would start sharing things then at one point as I went to sit my chair up, the back of the recliner caught my IV stand and knocked it over towards her.

With quick reflexes she caught it and when the nurses came over to check if everything was alright, she disappeared. I didn't see her the rest of my treatment. If that's not Creators way of telling me to shut up, like a parent being stern with their child to get the message across, I don't know what is!! Humbling to say the least.

Becoming willing….

The balance of survival and moving into the sacred space of Living is a life-long journey. We don't just arrive. At least I haven't yet. My hopes are that the times between hanging onto my ass for the alligators and truly breathing in the present moment without fear, anxiety or judgement will become farther and farther apart. Leaving my spirit in its well-desired place of peace and contentment. I essentially came out of the womb in survival mode.

Not putting blame anywhere. It has taken me many years of revisiting in and out of those times, but more layers have been healed. I can genuinely say with that sense of detachment that I used to judge others for that sounded like they were expressing their lack of compassion and denial that I agree with now.

It was never that for them, it was either they had also healed or simply it was their own survival mechanism that was keeping them safe." It was just the way it was" was the response to these external circumstances.

I learned to settle into this new way of evolving which was surrounded by events that held me without opportunity to joyfully discover Life. And that's ok too. The commitment I made with the good Creator would not reveal itself fully until after a succession of experiences that will propel me out of the comfort zone I have developed and become accustomed to.

The opportunity has always been there, once I became of the age that I started to make conscious decisions for myself despite not having a clear roadmap yet. As every event has transpired, I would as I shed light on previously, find that emotional, mental, and physical stance that would tether me to the ground until I could come out the other side. Fortunately, this methodology worked to help me arrive to this place and time, unfortunately I missed some of the key markers to add to my internal book of lessons. Teachings that could have helped me to expand that balanced space.

I was told early in Sobriety when I would share about the days where I traveled back to the very earliest of time to claim some sort of clarity and put the truth where it lay.

It was not my fault the traumatic events that were perpetrated unto me so how could I take responsibility for any part? My sponsor most compassionately responded "no you did not have a part to play in that but, how you let it affect your behavior today, that's where your responsible" Even now....

Since the last chemo cycle very recently, another piece of the puzzle has dropped into place for me. I realized that I stayed so busy in the needing to just get "through" life without living was not only because I had been afraid of living, but because of my fear of death. By staying busy outside of myself, choosing careers that were all about helping others took the focus off me and my inner transitional steps to a place of Being that is not an end but only a continuation on a different plain.

A couple weeks ago I finally started a will, did more purging of material stuff that I have been hanging onto for God knows why and how long. As I was going through the totes the memories both uncomfortable and fond alike flooded back at different moments. Along with the "what the heck was I thinking I would need this for" times. I discovered ironically that the more I put down into the will, the freer I started to feel inside. Freer to welcome life now.

This feeling was supported in a wonderful long-awaited visit with my good friend and Reiki Master Michelle. As we were catching up, exchanging bits and bobs of our past, she shared with me some about her own thoughts on how uncomfortable she had been with conversations about death until her Mother-in-law Wanja, her Reiki Master, mentioned how once she was able to plan her time of leaving that now she could just enjoy life. That, that part was out of the way to no longer encumber her. I woke this morning with this realization that I have a choice.

The cancer is now remission. Yes, I still need to do a lengthy oral program to extend the time it will not return which will hopefully lengthen my stay. However, I am totally free to choose how I will step into this next phase. Now we never really know how long we have anyways.
I can wholeheartedly focus on the idea of although I learned and grew and healed so much these last six months, I can either spend my energy wondering how much longer I have, which puts me completely back into survival mode, or, I can have the faith and courage to allow myself to LIVE. However, that looks without having to control what is not mine to.

This means finish the will, put it aside, allow myself the giving the gift daily to myself of Reiki., which is this most incredible Life Force Energy healing modality passed down to me through the direct lineage originating with Mikao Usui who after sitting in meditation discovered Reiki on Mt Kurama in Old Kyoto before going on to practise for 7 years.

Then his lineage successor Mr Hayashi became Hawayo Takata's Reiki teacher in the 1930s, who brought it to North America, teaching those that were put in her path. In 1979 one beautiful Soul was Wanya Twan, who during her much-loved time here taught others as well as her daughter-in-law.

My friend Michelle Beauregard whom through our own what seemed separate paths started to intertwine in the late 90's to create this most awe-mazing relationship of, friend, fellow star traveller, ceremonial sister, and my Reiki mentor/ master.

I give much gratitude that the Universe put us together again the other day. I was sharing with Her how over the years so many people would say to me that they were concerned about while doing Reiki on someone, that would I not pick up their wounded energy? I have repeatedly responded with "I am but a conduit or go between if you will of the Life Force Energy. I

will only receive what is of the highest vibration from those I sit with during this healing time." Early on in my teachings a small handful of us gathered to take our level 2 Reiki and this is where I learned the explanation. Not only did we get the practical part of the course, but we also had the opportunity to practice within the safety and kindness of Michelles space which always seemed to include a cat.

Whether it was hers or just a visitor, this feline spirit brought the balance of comfort and a knowing. Like an Elder keeping a silent watch on how the class was going to transpire. She would always find a way to become involved by either joining the participant that was on the table to receive during group reiki sessions or she would wander between our legs brushing up ever so slightly to let us know she was a part of the team.

To explain a bit further for context Level two encompasses the sending of Distance Reiki. Sending it to the past, present or even future situations whether they be Mental, Physical, Emotional, or Spiritual that arises. To anyone anywhere. At Michelles suggestion for a try-out we decided to send Reiki to the Dahli Llamas wellbeing. In the circle we assumed the posture most comfortable for us individually and proceeded.

Our hands, palm out in front of us about chest high. I closed my eyes and fell into the rhythm of my breath. I'm not sure how long we were in this state. About halfway through my upper body started to sway in almost a clockwise circular motion. This most blissful feeling of inner joy and contentment spread through me

Once we were done, we then took turns sharing how this experience was. I was still in my bliss. The fellow to my right started was sharing how in times past he'd had the opportunity to see the Dahli Llama in person and was familiar with his energy. He then continued about how his own body during the sending started to sway, he spoke almost word for word about what I had just felt, and I didn't even have my eyes open at any time to view his experience! Ok well that just confirmed the teaching.

Well, that's just perfect....

The timing of our connectiveness is all-ways the right time. Every experience both challenging and joyful. In 2013 I made the decision to venture once again out of my comfort zone of familiarity in work, play and community.

I hadn't been out of Canada since before 2006 and I was getting itchy feet. Even though home was comfort surrounded by others, when I traveled I would do so alone. People would say repeatedly "aren't you scared to go places like that by yourself? "And I would not hesitate to reply, "Nope as a matter of fact I preferred it that way." In being by myself I didn't have to albeit selfishly not have to work around anyone else's schedule, wants or needs.

I could be freer to follow my bliss, my hearts desire, I was able to have the freedom to tap in, when need be, to the teachings waiting to be shared from the Universe through the experiences I was having. This time my sights were set on Thailand. Chang Mai to be exact. I had decided to embark on yet another aspect of healing to add to my repertoire of modalities by learning Thai massage. I was initially going to take it in Whistler from an awesome woman who received her certification to teach in Thailand.

After researching flights, accommodations, and schooling I decided I was going right to the source. The plus side was it cost the same. Best decision EVER! Not only did it feed my exploring spirit, but I was also able to experience their summer to our winter, spend extra time once all my courses were done wandering the country sides in the rural communities. Fulfilling two of my desires.

One of these blessed places was a small village called Pai up in northern Thailand only accessible by a quick flight or if one was brave enough the 97-switchback drive where you are crammed into a van, hanging onto the inside wherever possible as you were tossed about like a loose bag of marbles.

Not a trip for the motion sickness sensitive. Which was what I turned out to be. I obviously wasn't the only one the driver had ever had on board as there was a designated stop site about a quarter of the way up for the purpose of regaining one's composure away from other passengers' laps so to speak. I vowed to take the flight back.

Once my schooling was complete and I survived the drive, my days consisted of having an early breakfast of watermelon, pineapple, and mango on a stick from a street vendor, then wander the area looking for the local temples. I was there three days when I came across one about an hour walk down a single lane of combined dirt and old paved road leaving Pai that beckoned me in. As I entered, my whole being released in a way that felt like a full body sigh.

Whatever I had unknowingly been carrying with me stayed at the door. Looking around for the place to sit I was immediately stuck by the décor if that's what it's called inside.

Imagine at the front where in a religious temple stood the pulpit for the minister, instead was a golden Buddha on a bit of a higher platform surrounded by offerings of flowers, lit candles, small plates of food and tiny cups of liquid.

From the belly of the Buddha protruded 5 white ropes which extended across the ceiling over another rope grid-like pattern. These ropes then made their way out an opening between the roof and the back wall into the village.

I learned later that these ropes were one continuous trail connected to every building regardless of what the building housed throughout the community joining every being to Source, to Buddha back at the temple. How cool was that!

Furthermore, inside the temple at every square in the grid from the ceiling dropped a small rope so that when you sat beneath it. If you chose you could move the hanging rope, so it touched your head to sit on your crown chakra. Its like you were plugged in as well while you prayed in your own way.

I was elated, calm, full of goosebumps and at home all at once if that's possible. I settled into my being, focusing on my breath, allowing the thoughts to flow in and out, I stopped at one. I realized the commonality of the belief behind the ropes in their way of existence was not unlike what an Elder walking the Red Road shared with me back home.

How they saw our connection to Creator. It was told to me that al the realms looks like that of a spider web, where in the center is the good Creator. Attached to Source are all the web strings which are the pathways that carry the ones that have come before us, those here now and those yet to come. These are seen as the little nodules at different intervals on the web lines. The whole premise is we are all connected.

I was once again reassured that the path I felt was guiding me was the right one. My whole trip was being one of just following intuition while being open to the signage posted. Even though I have the memories, some days it feels surreal that I was gifted with them. 4 days later I was blessed with achieving goal number two. Before I made my way to South America, I had always dreamed of talking, touching, being, feeling with an elephant.

Now Thailand is famous for many places to do so. Ranging from rescue reserves to over-populated touristy driven sanctuaries. Neither appealed to me so when I was yet on another one of my meandering's moments, I just put it out there to the Universe to guide me. I kid you not within about 20 minutes down at the end of a dirt road all by itself was this untethered Elephant looking in my direction swaying back and forth as if to say "here I am. I'm waiting for you."

I headed straight for Her. When I approached closer, she reached out with her trunk and started to air scent me, checking me out as it were.

Her size was a little overwhelming for me but once I looked into her big brown eyes lined with the most gorgeous lashes, I felt no harm would come. Yes, she had been expecting me.

It felt like long before I even hit the dirt road that morning she somehow knew. Once I was within touching distance her caretaker appeared out from behind her. He was bringing her a bunch of banana leaves for snack. We started to chat, and while he encouraged me to feed her some leaves, he told me her story. She had been orphaned at approximately 2 years of age when he came across her unwilling to leave her mothers body that had been attacked by mountain poachers, he knew he was meant to take care of her.

Her name was Baung Ma and she was now 42. He was able to provide for her well-being by offering rides into the fields and mountainside up the road from his place. I was more than happy to support his commitment to her. She idled up to the staired raised platform level with the height of her back and waited patiently for me to figure out how to climb on without sliding off the other side. She resonated so much tenderness and love, it was all I could do not to start crying.

She had a rope hanging very loosely around her neck which continued into a leash like apparatus. The caretaker also had in his hand a large metal hooklike item it which to guide her if warranted. Neither was needed at any time during the travels

. As a matter of fact, she was so secure in her purpose and feelings of familiarity and safety with him established by a long history of bonding, with me perched upon her that she just made her way along at her own gentle pace along the trails. Her footing was very precise and sure. Even when we would approach a downhill boulder covered section, she maneuvered her way effortlessly through it without disturbing my balance on top.

She would instinctively stop periodically. Allowing me to catch my breath and take a good look around bringing the view into my memory bank. She had the cutest wisps of course black and grey hairs about three inches long on her head. I rang my fingers around them in delight. I was in rapture. I kept leaning over her and hugging her, thanking her, giving her all the love in my heart. The kindness she showed me to this day still brings tears of gratitude and feelings of oneness that reaches far beyond the two-legged Ones we call our human relatives.

◆◆◆

I hear you calling....

Finding that sacred balance between living life and surviving is not just about letting go of thoughts, words and actions that no longer serve and support the transition but to also reflect. Share and continue all that contributes to success of the living side. This concept was never more evident then when I started on the Natural wellness path shared with me first through the original cultural teachings from Indigenous first peoples.

Their way of sharing in the bringing to light the ancient ways of the Plant medicine given to them by the Ancient Ones translated to them from Spirit. As my desire for the knowledge and connection to the Medicine grew, so did the circle of information that held it flourish. I will say that in my genuine exuberance to absorb it all in the fastest way possible, I had to be reminded time and again in many ways the importance of understanding and following the ways which had been lain out before me and those that came to show me.

There was, I discovered quite quickly a solid reason for the protocols in acquiring this sought after way of life. Once started, it wasn't to be just a hobby, a parttime interest to pick and choose how the path would be travelled.

With each encounter, I had to learn to listen, not just with my ears but with that energetic beacon that was designed to receive all that was being transmitted by the plants when switched to the on position.

This was not an easy process and so it made sense when my first Teacher shared with me that when we come onto this path it is important to only choose three plants we would like to study. Although some have only dedicated themselves and their quest to only one. This confused me at first because every time I ventured out into the forest, the plants homes, I was drawn to them all. I could hear them welcoming me in my heart, my arms would get goose bumps in 40-degree weather.

Individual bushes would wave noticeably while all around them was no sign of a breeze. It felt like this was where I was meant to be all my life, and possibly was there before in another one.

By adhering to this simple principle, it gave the time, space, and commitment to learn absolutely everything needed or at least everything the plant spirit was willing to share.

Which by the by can and has taken a lifetime for many. How to listen to the ones that call you that had been waiting to fulfill their commitment to their cycle of life has been an incredible experience time and again.

Not just the coincidental finding of the plants but how the spirits around would let me know when I was done harvesting. Many years ago, I was up in the sub-alpine with my then partner at the time and an Elder from the community of Cranbrook. The elder was honouring us with the opportunity to gather Bear root. Also known as Osha.

Its name was given long ago he explained because it is one of the very first plants a bear when coming out of hibernation instinctively consume. The amazing medicinal properties of this plant are that it clears out the not only the digestive tract of any stagnancy but also opens the bronchia in a way that supports the releasing of any mucus or viral and bacterial visitors to the lungs while reducing any inflammation in the respiratory tract.

 Osha  Artist Conk  Spirit portal

Great for our sleepy relatives to shake off anything hanging around and stimulate their body to start consuming food and water again. After doing the specific food and tobacco offering to the bear spirit, we started to gather. While doing so the Elder continued to share such great teachings about the plant, the difference between regular bear root and grizzly bear root, which up until then did not know there was more than one species. I had in the past been gifted and utilized this sacred plant and it was so good to learn more about it.

After a while I felt like I had harvested enough. My goal was to only take what would last for a couple years without being overly indulgent. I learned it was an important gathering practise to not go back to the same spot every time either. Give the plants a chance to replenish themselves. My partner was still feverishly hunting and digging and gathering when the Elder let us know the bear spirit was telling us we had enough, and it was time to leave the area. My partner decided to ignore him and kept on.

As the Elder and I made our way back to where we parked the car on the side of the logging road, I once again told my partner it was enough time to go. Just as I said that A wind from what seemed like nowhere picked up and a very sturdy bush beside the car started to shake. Around this bush all other aspects of the forest did not seem affected by the wind at all. After the third call out my partner begrudgingly made his way back to the car.

It was just in the nick of time in my opinion as once we three were in the vehicle the bush beside us was waving back and forth with an intensity that frankly scared me.

Then the car started to rock as well. The elder started laughing as we sped off. He than asked if we got the message. Yep! Needless to say with the performance of disrespect of my soon to be ex, I made the decision he would not accompany me on any future gatherings. In the beginning, I was constantly befuddled about how much of themselves they chose to give to me, especially when I didn't have a clue who would be receiving the healing. But as with all my experiences that part would make itself known at the right time.

There were many times I would have the shelves full but seemingly nowhere for them to go then someone would show up out of what seemed like nowhere that was searching, asking for help with a health issue.

Lo and behold here was the solution sitting on my Ikea shelf hidden behind a colourful sarong for a door to protect from the sunlight, with the information on the usage of it sitting within my Being. The humanness in me took some turns at different intervals going from Oh wow how cool am I which enabled the Creator to bring me back down to reality on a regular basis until I was finally able to remember I was not a Medicine person.

I can't allow the words of others to deny my truth that I am a student and will be so all my life. Once again, I am brought back to the understanding that even though this path was part of the commitment I had made before coming into this realm I was/am still just a conduit of Source. The time of only focusing on helping others has just been meant to be part of the process.

There is so much more to this way of working with the medicines after the offerings are given. The prayer of intentions and humbly asking for approval and guidance to completing the Plants transition into the processing, storing, and distribution is just as much a sacred aspect of the process as the gathering itself and must be carried out with a clear and humble heart. For we are still but the vessel in which the medicines honouring its own journey happens.

Hope growing from compassion....

The times have occurred during these last few years, most especially the last 6 months that to close the cycle and be in the presence of the wellness within, I had to now apply all the many ways I had learned to my own personal inward journey going back to pull away and gently lay to rest the next layers that I inadvertently glossed over being in survival mode.

As I started to be willing to ask for help from the people that Creator sent to support me, the plethora of medicines specific to my physical needs to accompany the western ways appeared in an abundance that blew my mind. Made my heart cry, causing me to forever be in a state of gratitude.

The lessons through events I have interacted with are only the means to honor this closing of the cycle does not mean a physical death into the next realm but if learned in the way that propels my steps forward in a good way, I am becoming my authentic Self residing truly in the heart of the Living. It's been a couple weeks now since the last chemo treatment wrapping up the last six months of intensive moment to moment treatments. Already that aspect of the journey feels like a lifetime ago.

A string of hours, days, moments woven in amongst each other without at times a semblance of rationality interrupted with dashes of periodic profound Ah Ha episodes. I do not take as a surety that every event, teaching, and memory as I understand them is the final word so to speak. That there is nothing more to reveal itself to explain the rationale for walking through it.

That would be just way too much ego in play on my part to believe that. I feel like the only reason I was able to have those moments of clarity was because of the various layers of understandings that would expose themselves only when I was ready.

These moments have transpired from the various teachings I have been a part of in all areas of my life since I was traumatically pulled out of the only physical space that was my world for a time, my mothers' womb.

She had been mutilated with a long-standing birthing procedure called a cesarian section. Today I understand the depth of feelings of violation she must have felt during that time. The surgery that was to save my life recently which I underwent to remove all of cancer visitor within my abdomen is how I can relate.

This process could only be done by a very similar means in which slicing open my abdomen and digging through the underlying layers of what has protected the inner workings of me. The rummaging around, pushing aside for better access with an intensity in hopes of finding every speck. Not unlike digging through the sock drawer tossing the pairs aside to find that one lone match to the one in the hand.

The order of contents is now forever altered. No matter how carefully, and with the greatest intentions and skill, will it be the same again. It is changed. I have changed as a result, on all levels of my being. Does one spend time wishing for the old ways in which the contents were in the place you left them the last time you visited the drawer? Or does one decide that acceptance, with an understanding of the change.

The willingness to approach said drawer with a new perspective based on what is now, not what was while knowing that every time the drawer is opened there will be opportunity to view and learn from the layer that now presents itself. The surgery not only physically altered my inner contents but mentally, emotionally, and spiritually did so. So, every time my mind travels back to that and the six months surrounding it, the view is/will be different. The feelings, the thoughts attached to each visit will hopefully have a broader, a more encompassing healing perspective.

That the scars lain down will lose the raw, swollen painful redness and eventually become the slightly different skin toned color of the experience of a warrior. The kind of warrior that can walk openly, in vulnerability, peaceful within. Offering up the map to the steps taken without donning exterior layers of protection called anger, fear, or insecurity.

For now, I am not there, but this is my hope. I NEED this hope. My spirit craves it.
For with this hope, it allows me to put one foot in front of the other when the only way through to the other side of the moment is to reach into the other drawer that is also my tools to survive by drawer and pull out the hope tube of goo and fill the cracks of despair.

Love my Relatives….

For the past two years I have had the privilege of being visited quite regularly by all sorts feathered friends, squirrels, both black and grey and the occasional mother/son raccoon duo. These relatives have been such a blast. Watching their unique individualized characteristics presenting themselves at any given time has indeed been some of the highlights of my days. The way they look at me when I greet them seeming like they understand the sounds coming out of my face.

Almost from the time they first introduced themselves to me I started presenting the offerings of their foods of choice and yes, I say choice because the ones that visit the birdfeeder buffet seem to have different taste palates.

For instance, it doesn't seem to matter what the birdseed package says or who it was geared towards, they have their preferences. They will systematically binge on the seeds they want while tossing what they think is the lesser of out of the feeder onto the ground at the same time. Now that's some great foraging skills right there!

The crows on the other hand, in the beginning were happy with anything I put out there. From leftover panfried potatoes to sliced up Ukrainian sausage that was reduced to clear from the discount section at the store down the road. Having said that there was one pair, I assume they were a couple based on how they would show up together, offering up themselves to their significant other for the per functionary grooming before perching themselves outside my kitchen window in a way that gave them the best view inside to gain my attention. It was like they're saying "where are you. We're here for snack".

As soon as I spot them, I greet them with a cheery good morning, asking them if it's snack time. In response They will cock their head to the side looking right at me! As time has gone on though these two have made it very clear that they prefer whole grain bread chunks to plain dinner rolls. Will scramble over each other for the hamburger crumbs from the left-over pasta sauce. One black beauty started to extend its trust in me by taking food right from my fingers. but of course, only if I stayed perfectly still, arm outstretched, with my head turned away so the involuntary movement of my eyes wouldn't scare it.

Now I say it because I'm still not sure which one this was. Every once in awhile I thought I had it figured out based on different characteristics like the size seemed smaller than the others and a white, which I can only assume was a poop stain on its wing. But then after I would go through this successful ritual with, I shall call it Steve, then suddenly wouldn't matter what I was offering or how long I stayed in the required position, Steve wouldn't take the offering. Turns out there was more than one Steve that fit the description!

The squirrels, they've taken a little longer to figure out. I know there are three black squirrels and two greys because at certain times I've seen them all together chasing each other in a spiral motion up and down the massive trunks of the two cedar trees along the back fence. Or when I started to spread the bird seed out over the stone slates which the landlady installed to replace the grass, they've tried to gather as much as they could in between the darting about of the various wee winged ones.

 After a year and a half there is one grey squirrel that will cautiously make its way to my porch area perching on his hind legs long enough to track the Brazil nut I toss as close to him as possible before darting in , snapping it up , giving it the once over to make sure it is in fact a treat before scurrying off into the undergrowth of the surrounding plant life. I started going outdoors to present the treat when I would see it feeding on the seeds but would become confused and I'll admit a bit disappointed when for some reason it would B-line for the nearest getaway spot when I opened the door instead of coming towards me.

Well, turns out not the same fuzzy friend. I started to catch on and decided to only come out the door with the treat when I saw through the same kitchen window the squirrel approaching my door. Otherwise, I finally quit chasing him and the other nonhuman creatures. It only took a year and a half.

Figuring it out....

Sometimes I'm not the brightest Crayola in the package. Other times I know, but I don't want to know, so I pretend I don't know......You know! I am however in this moment in time feeling like I am not "in the know". The days are blending into one and other to the point I'm having to consciously remind myself which one I am in.

Am not quite up to strength to do the long walks, go to the ocean, long drives or anywhere to do anything that requires more than and hours physical investment without a good nap to follow up . I am realizing how extremely small my world has become. Seclusion and quiet is not all it's cracked up to be I'm finding. I can only have so much screen time, snack time, or alone time in my head. Am feeling restless.

Questioning myself, Creator If this is all there is left. Did I just go through the last life altering experience just to be alone in my home, head, and heart? One would think that with experiencing such a challenging event that was Cancer, that there would be this clear alternative, life changing path emerging that will make a difference in at the very least the world as I know it around me.

What's next, do I just fade away meaningless into the background? My sons have now seemingly reverted to their status quo. It's like now that they know I'm ok, there is not the daily texts asking how I'm doing or the offering up moments of their time to get together. This is most definitely alright with me because I would assume that's a good thing. It means they are not worried anymore about losing me and can now take the time to breathe and live their lives as they are meant to.

Afterall they, just like me have their own commitments with the good Creator that they are honouring. I will admit even though it is important they do so, there is a small selfish part of me that thought at least this experience that had brought us closer together would last forever which is what I have wanted for so long. My mother in her woundedness managed to push away everyone that ever cared about her. Her reactionary behaviors were so painful to receive that I had to remove myself from the firing line.

I vowed all my life I would not be like her and for a long time now I haven't at least not that I am aware of. Many years in fact. Even so when I am still enough, I catch a glimpse of the times past when I was. Those viewings stir up guilt within that feels like it wouldn't matter how much time I have left; I could never make it up to my boys and feel their forgiveness. This creates fear within. Feelings of purposelessness. The desire and urgency to help others without being asked, lavishing my boys with all sorts of goodies whether it be all my food from the freezer, supplements that I know they take, or random items from the Thrift stores I frequent.

When I am amid these actions, I somehow believe I am proving I am worthy of the original Love. It has become my way of keeping the lines of communication open, especially with my boys. When the line goes silent however, I automatically think they are mad at me for something. What did I do? What did I say?

So, I stew on that idea for a few moments, sometimes hours (used to be days) run all sorts or scenarios through with the gamut of emotions attached to each scene. I'll distract myself by heading back to the thrift stores or grocery shops under the pretense of wanting something. It is true I do have a desire; I need the human connection of being out where others are. Making the sudden eye contact while passing each other in the isle.

Starting up a brief casual conversation about absolutely nothing. Seeing the old familiar faces of the cashiers or other employees. Hearing their greeting even though it is part of their protocol, brings about I'm sure the same feelings inside that Norm from that long ago sitcom "Cheers" felt when he would enter the bar, and everyone shouted" Norm!"

I feel seen. It's my social time. All that I have imagined to be going on in my head dissipates for a bit until I am back home again and watch the news about some event whether be a tragedy or a good feel happening. I will then finally have a cry, get honest with myself about where its all coming from then ask Creator for help.

All this happens within me, with the Me, Myself, and I committee to figure it out. I need to cut that out. I have begrudgingly decided to utilize the counselling services provided by the Cancer Society. I have had much success transitioning through times of mental, emotional, and spiritual suffering in the past. I will not find the calmness of mind and heart that is what some call peace from Instagram reels or Facebook posts no matter how much I scroll.

This only leads me to the temporary illusion all's ok again followed by more isolation and feelings of screwed uppedness. At the end of the day no matter how much I want to reach out and share what's really going on inside on the ole media platforms, that is not the place. It is not real. I used the excuse for quite awhile during lockdown that it was the only way I could stay in contact with those I love but since Covid, it has done the exact opposite.

It has, I have created a further divide of sorts. It feels like I've almost lost the ability to re-connect face to face, exchanging the essential vibrations that can only happen within physical proximity of another living Being. As for the daily repetitiveness and somewhat, ok not just somewhat, mundane lifestyle right now, I am extremely bored which has proven itself time and again to be a very dangerous place to be. It happens subtly in that I will start binge watching a succession of shows that are not healthy for my mind.

Shows that have a common theme to them about detectives and mysteries and crime. I recognize when I've had enough because I start having the weirdest dreams. I become agitated more easily at that new jar of spaghetti sauce that won't open. I get all weepy on a half hour sit-com that has a touchy-feely moment in it. I then start questioning the most obscure. I need to trust the process once again.

Trust that just because I can't see it happening, the next step evolving, that doesn't mean it's not. There is a reason I don't know and even though I think I know what that is, it's quite possible I don't. For now, however, I am being beckoned by the Crow. It's snack time for both him and me. That, I do know.

Stories shared....

It's interesting how at times during my video chats with my Pappy that when he tells me for the 3rd time in as many conversations about how their pup is so smart that she can find the car no matter what path they took walking away from it or to return, I automatically think it's because he is 87 years old and had a stroke just a few years ago, or maybe it's the starting of dementia or Alzheimer's?

Do I fear I'm slowly losing the precious time we have left together? So, I commit to asking him more about his life, about the various experiences he had in so many fields. Holy man he has done so much and been in so many different places! Maybe that's where I get the roaming, lets try another new thing I've never done before Gene ...

My logical self tells me "The way he is going, he will outlast us all!" This man is awe-inspiring. The simple way he puts one foot in front of the other to get to the next step in whatever is happening in his moment.

Then I found myself being reminded by my oldest son not that long ago when sharing with him about something that It seems I've told him already. I'm pretty sure I'm not losing my mind. This repetitive behavior I now understand is my way, meaning myself and maybe Pappys?

A Way of wanting to create strong connections, re-enforce bonding and share our love, be part of their lives as they seem to grow more distant by rightfully participating fully in their own lives.

However, its possible the other day I was going for a walk, when it felt like there was someone following me and yet no one was there so I just spoke out loud to whoever the spirit was, "if you are not sent by the good Creator then you need to leave. Back to the light."

If someone witnessed me seemingly talking to myself, maybe, just maybe they might have thought I was not completely of sound mind.

Another sign my world has progressively become so much smaller is there's not a lot of outside stimuli or a varied degree of daily events that happen. There was a time when I removed myself from other peoples lives or created a larger distance because I had this fear of being so very vulnerable which is my authentic self and end up getting hurt.

For a while now though this self-made boundary is a result of just not wanting the vibration of any more drama, head games, gossip or complaining that when exposed long enough, sticks to my aura like Velcro. So, when I talk about my day and what's happening in it, there is only a select few topics to talk about. It is all I have. It makes sense that the stories are on repeat. Hmm...I'm seeing a resemblance in not just my Pappys life, but to all the lives I've crossed where the theme is the same. I can see and understand now how easy it is to pick up those drama creating tools without realizing it.

The wish to feel that adrenaline bubble through the veins letting one know somethings about to happen. Back in the day our moments were so busy with finding the hunting and gathering of food or medicine source by relocating to follow the herds, the Sun, the Moon cycles that there was no such thing as these time-wasting activities.

When there was down time so to speak the opportunity was immediately pounced on by using the time for the trading of treasured items only found in the giver's territory or the sharing of stories to keep culture and the tribes accounts of historical wisdom and beliefs. Stories that held our past, the vast knowledge of the wisdom keepers who by their own right held a sacred place amongst us.

This was how we survived. Being on the look out for the many ways in which to keep our lineage alive. Today there still is this innate desire to stay connected with other social beings. We/I do this by relating to another's day. I do this when given the opportunity, acknowledging their experience they share by retrieving a similar one from my memory bank.

Then, when it is my turn, I present it. I have been known however to be in such a hurry to create that bond that I inexcusably interrupt them with my tale.

As if to say, "I can totally relate to what's happening in your world because I felt the same way when this happened in mine." By doing this it feels like there is this comradery that has been established which re-affirms my existence. I think I can understand maybe just a bit now about why some appear to be stuck in the I remember when loop because there is no new data from present day to mix it up. It is slowly happening to me.

The goal is to find the balance. I had a Facebook memory pop up today from over 8 years ago when I was in my glory waist high in recycling that needed to be sorted. The first feeling about this memory was that of nostalgia, followed by a yearning for that simpler time contributing to the welfare of the community I lived in. Clearing up the wreckage of our presence in some small way.

I thought until my one of my sisters commented "Working with you when I visited as a teenager still has me obsessed with improving waste management systems".

Tears immediately started streaming down my face, sobs were coming up from my chest. Deep moving emotions of gratitude. So very grateful that if my whole life of action and thought created this opportunity for her, for the future, then I haven't failed in purposefulness however minute I think I am. Maybe I'll take up a part time volunteer job. I know my limits though and wouldn't be able to handle working at the SPCA. I'd want to take every relative home.

It would just be too sad for my heart. My Pappy has the same emotions. When I was a teenager, he said it was ok for me to get a small dog for companionship so off to the pound we went. We weren't in there very long before my Pappy told me he would wait outside until I was done choosing. I think he said it was all the barking, but his eyes were misty as he left. Up and down the small cages on the shelves I wandered.

Neither Dad nor I liked the yappy ones so that was narrowing the choices down. At the very end of the row, I saw her. She was this little fox Terrier/ Chihuahua cross. She was sitting very still seemingly resigned to her fate. There was this look on her face that said "well if you take me, you take me. If you don't you don't." For some unknown reason I felt that. Maybe she was the mirror to my already sorely wounded soul. I can't say, but she was the one. It took a few days of her being with us before I named Snoopy. It was quite fitting.

Not only because she was black and white but because one of the first days she was in the yard, feeling the fresh air and playing in the grass, she suddenly started crawling across the grass on her stomach scratching it I think, and I had this immediate flashback to a snoopy cartoon strip where He was doing that very same thing.

At the time I didn't know the story yet of how Snoopy came to Charlie Brown, so I was unaware of the resemblance there. Snoopy was such a smart, funny charismatic Pup. When I think of her, my heart still swells. (insert many heart emojis here)

Sharing is caring....

I had the most awesome day yesterday with a wonderful friend. We attended the widely coveted 60th year CHFA (Canadian Health Food Association) tradeshow event in Vancouver! It was so good to see long time friends from the industry that I have made over the years and had the opportunity to make new ones. We put in over 8000 steps according to my fitbit!! And we still didn't see every booth. It was just so great to get out into the real world. To share it with a like-minded of sorts.

I have become so accustomed to venturing out into unknown spaces in time by myself most of my life that I will admit every now and again the urge to just mosey on without her got the best of me and I had to remind myself to wait or turn back.

Not a bad thing in fact was a good awareness as to my state of Being and that there is a spark of desire to explore the possibilities of sharing adventure space another time. Yay for growth!

At the end of the day when I dropped her off at her abode, my heart flushed with such appreciation and love for this beautiful woman that journeyed with me today. We had worked together at my last job; she resigned not long after I was let go. A couple times during our excursion today we affirmed with others that even though that job had its issues with us both what it did however was create an opportunity which we took to enter a longer lasting awesome friendship that will survive long after the memory of the job.

The day was such that I was given the gift to share parts of the last chapter in my life's story to date. Each time I shared with a distributor or Rep. I was not only welcomed and supported by them but I also felt stronger, stronger in the feeling that in the not so distant future when I enter back into the wellness field that is my passion, my calling, I want to specialize in supporting and help those that have had a similar experience navigate what can seem quite overwhelming with information and choices for continued healing day to day.

I have been in and around this industry for 18 years and I have seen firsthand that there is like so many other professions those that are in it for the quick buck and those that genuinely care deeply in what they do.

I don't profess to have all the answers, nor can I guarantee fixed outcomes including in my own journey, but I can however share my experience, strength, and hope that I have with those that ask. I feel like every experience I have I can process it a couple of ways.

I can see it as an opportunity to learn and grow while refining my purpose or I can slowly melt into the background in a way that creates more pain within myself and others. In just 4 more days I am relocating the mind, body and spirit to a wonderous new opportunity of exploration, growth and re-connection in the most authentic way with all that is pure, original and welcoming.

Through this last but not the LAST page of my story I have had to make many adjustments in the way of letting go. My income has dropped to one third of what it was only a short time ago which has forced me to give up present housing. I would hazard a guess to say I have had to release at least two-thirds of my household contents. So grateful for rubber maid totes though. I have rummaged, sorted and selected. I have traveled the map of memories attached while carefully selecting what's left of my past present and future, placing them gently into the blue bins.

I have been working relentlessly hard on not allowing what now has seemed to be the most prominent fear of ending up homeless. The fear that has been vying for 1st place over the pre-existing one of this physical life coming to an end that has on occasion dominated my thoughts, my verbiage when asked how I am doing. Unfortunately, I am not unique in this situation either. I am not special. Nor am I a victim.

This reality of my situation reflects the direction the world has been pointed in for a long time now due to the human's inability to be content with what is in all present moments, the constant blind focus on the illusion that more, more of everything and the means to achieve it without regard to the ripple effect it creates while trying to attain it, is more important. (I include myself in this category).

Without physical evidence before me that the path going forward would continue to be safe, clear and most importantly where I am meant to be, it has forced me to once again dig deep into the ancient wisdom of what I know to be true in that I will/am ok. I am continuing to be in the greatest of care of the Creator, Source of Life. The visible steps before me are shown based on my degree of willingness to have this trust.

So.... what has been revealed is in just a few more sleeps I will be leaving the concrete jungle called the lower mainland and starting anew on a small island between here and Vancouver Island. A quiet community called Mayne Island.

Annnd I'm back on the mainland within two weeks of that island experience. OMG is all I will say! So grateful for past life lessons that taught me about red flags.

Even though I am presently now without stable housing and after most recent scans, it looks like the visitor has not only returned, but decided to bring a friend and hang out in the accommodation that I call the liver. I am feeling like once again I am thrown back to the beginning of this latest journey.

All in all, I still feel Creator still has plans for me. He has heard my hearts yearnings. He has answered a couple very desperate ones I have lifted to Him on my own behalf through the most generous and unselfish act of a dear compassionate, authentic loving Being I am blessed to call my friend. I will call her an Angel even though she goes by Nada, has offered me a space in her and her family's life, their property, a blessed airstream to re-compose, get stronger and have a safe, nurturing place to find my footing again on the other side of what has been an all-consuming lengthy event this last year.

Most would say this is such a huge act of kindness and yes, I would agree but this act is not unlike so many others Nada has carried out in what seems like a lifetime I have known her. My memory is unclear as to the exact how's and when's our lives started to intertwine as it seems to me like it has always been this way. Some of my first reflections are of when I worked for her at what was the best (and I'm not just saying that because of our relationship) local Health food store called Be Natural Apothecary.

It was in downtown Pemberton BC in the shopping area that consisted of 2 whole blocks side by each. The moment one entered this most sacred space; their hearts told them they were in the right place. The mingled scents of essential oils, bulk herbs mostly wildcrafted from locally sourced companies, organic fresh fruits and vegetables with a hint of a newly born Soul that had come into this realm lightly awakened their ancient senses.

Nada created effortlessly an environment that welcomed all. From the first timers seeking information on how to add a supplement or two to their daily regime to those that had committed their wholistic journey within the shelves of this healthy haven as a way of life. I had finished my education becoming certified as a Natural Health Practitioner just a few years earlier topping up the already seemingly full resume of the old ways of education.

This amazing woman shared unselfishly with me through the wise ones whilst in their classroom that was Mother Nature when Nada welcomed me without question into her business fold.

 We became fast friends as she allowed my OCD, my still very unsure feelings of whether I was who she thought I was and creative processes to make themselves at home in her store while I slowly evolved to figure it out so to speak. I had already been welcomed and accepted into the community of Mt Currie and now here was an opportunity to bring a further connection, relationship if you will to the two communities that although were side by side, there was the unwritten wall of pain and distrust and rightly so that lay between them.

 Over the years though despite this veil members of Mt Currie started to seek out more and more the knowledge, genuineness and experience of Nada and her approach to all living Beings as a trusting truth.

 Including myself. She had created such a safe space that I was able to delve deeper into my instinctual, and the ancestral ways of applying the cultural Spiritual path that had opened to me through the trusted elders of Mt Currie that my footsteps were becoming much surer on. Her way of being her authenticity has not wavered in any way over the years.

Not only have I been touched by Nada, if one pays attention within the communities her fingerprints are lightly dusted upon so many others. For this I am truly grateful.

I feel this time coming will fulfill my need to also be in a setting volunteering where others and I would benefit from the teachings or lessons of my past while being the student once more in a balanced way. In time, find that job situation that will expose me to opportunities to create new friendships, new contacts, new stories.

If its in the Universes plans, I'll keep you in the know how I've achieved that. Until then I will continue to muddle along regaling you with one more "and then there was the time…"

Thank you for listening, I love you!

Manufactured by Amazon.ca
Bolton, ON